SOUTH
of the
HILL

GRACE BOYKIN

South of the Hill

Copyright © 2024 by Grace Boykin. All rights reserved.

No part of this publication may be reproduced, stored in a retrieval system or transmitted in any way by any means, electronic, mechanical, photocopy, recording or otherwise without the prior permission of the author except as provided by USA copyright law.

The opinions expressed by the author are not necessarily those of URLink Print and Media.

1603 Capitol Ave., Suite 310 Cheyenne, Wyoming USA 82001
1-888-980-6523 | admin@urlinkpublishing.com

URLink Print and Media is committed to excellence in the publishing industry.

Book design copyright © 2024 by URLink Print and Media. All rights reserved.

Published in the United States of America
Library of Congress Control Number: 2024922674
ISBN 978-1-68486-962-6 (Paperback)
ISBN 978-1-68486-967-1 (Hardback)
ISBN 978-1-68486-963-3 (Digital)

21.10.24

TABLE OF CONTENTS

Preface v
Chapter 1   Opening the Door to the Past 1
Chapter 2   Days of Darkness 5
Chapter 3   The Beginning 11
Chapter 4   House on 'the Hill' 16
Chapter 5   The 'Hunt' for Federal Funds 23
Chapter 6   Not Quite Politics as Usual 27
Chapter 7   "Kings" of the Hill 33
Chapter 8   The Telegram That Changed History 39
Chapter 9   Upheavals of the 1940s 44
Chapter 10   A Close Call 49
Chapter 11   Durability 61
Chapter 12   A Dream Comes True 66
Chapter 13   The Movie Deal 73
Chapter 14   Labor 100
Chapter 15   U.S. Role with China 111
Chapter 16   Fabulous Frank 134
Chapter 17   Affirmatives and Upheavals 137
Chapter 18   Power Struggles 148
Chapter 19   JFK's Speech to the Gridiron Club 166
Chapter 20   Gerrymandering 172
Chapter 21   The Black Day 178
Chapter 22   Burglaries 190
Chapter 23   End of an Era of 'Love' in Congress 202
Chapter 24   Post Commentaries 212
Resolutions 214
Harry F. Byrd, for President Frank W. Boykin, for Vice President 216

PREFACE

This story is a work inspired by the real life of the hardworking Frank W. Boykin, who demonstrated, developed, and was determined to devote every day of his life to city, state, nation, family, and friends. He gave God credit for all his successes.

He was a man of letters—long, effusive letters that rival the richest ingredients in *Little Orphan Annie*, *Sonnets from the Portuguese*, or a popular TV commercial. His correspondences include Winston Churchill, Harry S. Truman and other prominent and powerful figures. These letters document a rich part of American history told firsthand as it was unfolding.

Congressman Frank W. Boykin was elected to Congress from the First Congressional District of Alabama at a special election held on July 30, 1935, to fill the vacancy caused by the resignation of the Honorable John McDuffie. Mr. Boykin had been re-elected each time since 1935 and at the expiration of the eighty-fourth Congress, would have been in Congress over twenty-eight years. He had opposition in nine of his campaigns, and his greatest victory was carrying each of his seven counties, some of them by eighty percent of the vote. Mr. Boykin was well-known not only in his home state of Alabama and in Washington, but throughout the nation. He was especially known for his famous slogan: "Everything Is Made for Love." He truly lived his slogan, as he loved his fellow man.

Mr. Boykin was a self-made man. He came up the hard way. He started out at the age of eight as a water-boy with a railroad to help support a large family and got most of his early education from his teacher at night. He was prominently identified with real estate, timber, timber products, farming, cattle-raising and shipbuilding. He was an ardent conservationist both of game and natural resources. He and his associates reforested thousands of acres of cut-over land and planted over seven million pine seedlings in his lifetime. He owned a famous game preserve about forty-five miles north of Mobile, Alabama, called McIntosh, Alabama. For nearly forty years, he had some of the people of our country hunting on his preserve. He was a great lover of animals, especially dogs, and had rescued scores of them from the district pound and shipped them to friends all over the U.S.

Prior to the reorganization of Congress, he was a member of seven House Committees. He was very active on the Rivers and Harbors Committee, Public Buildings and Grounds Committee, Merchant Marine, Fisheries Committee, and was Chairman of the House Patents Committee. Frank was also on the House Veterans Affairs Committee. He sponsored a bill clarifying patent and trademark legislation, which is still referred to all over the world as the Boykin Act.

Set against the ever-changing, dramatic backdrop of the capitol and historic events that occurred in the United States during his lifetime, Frank Boykin's story is about twenty-eight years of serving as a United States congressman.

Many magazine articles, newspaper articles, congressional records, monuments and landmarks remain to remind us of Frank's legacy in Washington and the state of Alabama, which he loved dearly.

Another generation learns through personal letters, radio, magazines, newspapers, telegrams, and presently television about our great politicians. If you are fortunate enough to have a current or past member of your family who is a politician, you will have a better understanding of the sacrifice they make.

Grace Boykin, in her middle age, has been very busy siphoning through years of documents and ledgers dating back to 1918-1965 to write this book.

This book is dedicated to the life of Frank W. Boykin, James Robert Boykin, Starr Boykin, Jason, Boykin, Veda Sheaffer, Anna, Hannah, Amanda, Olson and the Boykin family and many generations to come.

FRANK BOYKIN IN HIS OFFICE IN WASHINGTON, D.C.

CHAPTER ONE

Opening the Door to the Past

I flew in from Tampa, Florida, to Gulfport, Mississippi. From there, I would make the little-over-an-hour-drive to Alabama, my home state. It's where my ancestors lived. Where my family still has stakes. Where my roots—and most of my memories—are.

Tell anyone on the East Coast that you come from "the South" and certain images seem to spring to mind government corruption, a failing education system, racism. Admittedly, Alabama has seen its share of troubles and has made some amazing strides. What I didn't realize was the whole history—the personal stories *behind* the state's progress—and how my family name is inextricably linked to the labor struggles, to the wars, and even to the Klan. For better. For worse. Forever.

But I was about to find all that out.

My father, Bob, and my sister, Starr (the butterfly of our family), were the first faces I saw at the airport. They were my ride across the state line to Alabama. My link back home. Knowing my background as a former history teacher, my sister turned to me halfway through the trip and said, "I found some files you should go through."

"What are they?"

"Old file cabinets from Papa."

I found myself growing anxious, wondering what on earth my grandfather could have saved. "Where did you find them?" I asked.

"I was rummaging through the old red barn—through the dust and cobwebs, checking to see what improvements needed to be done. There

I was, dripping with sweat, when I looked into a dark corner and some boxes caught my eye." Did I mention that Starr is also the drama queen of our family?

"So, I walked over and asked the caretaker, Chubby, to wipe the cobwebs off," she continued. "Then we carried them to the doorway, loaded them in the truck and brought them over to the old slave house... you know, where the teenagers stay. I glanced inside but didn't have the time to digest what was in them. Anyway, I figured you'd want to get first crack at them."

She gave me a smile as if she'd discovered some secret map marking a hidden treasure. And maybe she was right. But I also knew that history has a way of hiding secrets. Of enclosing skeletons in the family closet, where perhaps they're best kept. I had no idea what I'd find—and no way of turning away now that I was hooked.

Shortly after arriving at our dad's 'log cabin' in Double Gates, Alabama, Starr left to return home to Mobile. That left just me and my father—and decades of history for us to uncover.

But first there was the scenery for me to take in, which is itself a little slice of heaven. My father's 'cabin' is around 5,000 square feet with an indoor swimming pool on the property adjacent to the cabin, a pond in front and a wraparound porch. Many friends and family members would fish the pond from the porch or dock using cane poles for brim, or a spinning wheel or fly fish for bass.

The cabin houses many historic pistols, muskets, shotguns and rifles, as well as hundreds of turkey callers given to my father by the manufacturers or the creators of these works of art. Though part-museum in that respect, some rooms can be mistaken for a zoo, featuring mounted animals from around the world: kudos, elk, jaguars, bears, rattlesnakes and jackals, to name a few. The lodge on the hill is also home to taxidermy turkeys, ducks, white tail deer, and other animals hunted on the property.

Our family has a ninety-nine-year lease on the log cabin, which is situated about five yards from the white Colonial antebellum plantation house on the hill. It was built in 1905 and is surrounded by an 8,000-acre hunting preserve (which constitutes its own town of Double Gates,

Alabama, named within the last ten years) owned by the Boykin family. Though the plantation house is perfectly gorgeous, family members only seem to ever use it during hunts and Dad prefers staying in his cabin.

Just before the sun fell completely in the sky, so that there was a little daylight left with which to see, I went to the stifling hot 'guest house' on the property, which my sister informed me now held the files. It was an ex-slave house, complete with rusty tin roof and maybe two rooms, in total.

The land around it is densely populated by cypress trees, pinewoods and oak trees bedecked with swooping streamers of Spanish moss. Pecans had fallen from the trees, littering the ground like a carpet of brown wooden beetles, and I heard them crunch beneath my feet as I made my way inside.

Suddenly, the fresh outside air, perfumed with the sweet scent of magnolia blossoms, gave way to an overpowering humidity as the door closed behind me.

I walked right up to the cabinet file and creaked open the drawer. The first thing that surprised me as I rifled through the papers was how old the documents really were. There were files dating all the way from 1918 to 1965. And they were intact. It was a coup! World wars. The industrial age. The growing pains of our country. All documented by hand as they were unfolding. I was excited to find myself in my element, totally absorbed in years of forgotten, untold history.

But the few electric lights and the blistering heat in the guest house soon drove me out. I gathered however many files I could carry in my arms and took them to my father's cabin. Diving into history is one thing. Reliving it without electricity and air conditioning is quite another.

When Dad saw what I was holding, he let out a sigh. "Papa's letters," he said wistfully.

"More than that, Dad. There's page after page, letter after letter… documents and correspondences with what looks like everyone who was ever on Capitol Hill."

Dad shook his head in amusement. He knew his father, the congressman, was a colorful man, known on Capitol Hill and across the nation for his lengthy, jovial and factual letters to statesmen and friends alike. With this bounty of information, his life was an open book—and his biography was suddenly laid out on the table before us.

    I picked up one document at random to read. It repulsed me at first glance—the familiar letters: the curly "K," followed by another and then another. It could be none other than the Ku Klux Klan. I couldn't look away, as so many others did at that time, and before I knew it, one of the ugliest parts of our country's history came to life again in front of me...

CHAPTER TWO

Days of Darkness

The following letter was handwritten to Frank W. Boykin's personal secretary, Alphonse Lucas, on January 22, 1958. It came from Brownville, Kentucky.

My Dear Alphonse:
 The enclosed cartoons struck receptive chords in my nature and mind, and I thought it might also be of interest to you. I clipped them from the Louisville papers, both of which are well gotten up and edited.
 I am glad to see the Indians lining up with the Anti-Klan element of the South and helping us redeem the South from the east upon her by the activities of the Klan, which unfortunately seems to be cursed by these frequent recurrences and acts of the Ku Klux Klan. I have fought that crowd bitterly ever since the group at Gulfport raised its ugly head in the early 1920s and insulted me by inviting me to attend its organization meeting in the First Baptist Church at 8 P.M. one night in that early period and to cap the climax the invitation came from the Baptist minister. He was shrewd enough not to tell me what the purpose of the meeting was, just mentioned the fact that he was inviting a group of the leading men of Gulfport interested in the Civic welfare of the city. I was never so angry in my life as when he finished his introduction of the purpose of the meeting with the statement that it was to form a chapter of the Ku Klux

Klan. I immediately arose and denounced the whole thing in very vigorous language. So much so that two of my friends who were there said they did not imagine I could get so angry and speak so forcibly. At the end, I apologized for my presence, stating that I had had no intimation of what the purpose was, and in excusing myself I warned them that I would fight their Klan to my very last breath.

As for Eisenhower I can only say that what I predicted in my 4-page letter to Frank a few days before the election of 1952 has been verified. You may have the letter in the files or may recall having read it.

I have spent most of the past 5 months up here in Kentucky checking 19000 acres of mineral leads and will be here most of the time for the next 3 months before I finish.

Sorry I could not have been with you more frequently and for longer intervals during the vacation season. But I greatly enjoyed the meetings we had.

Please give my kind remembrances to Clatie and with the best of wishes and warmest regards for you, I am sincerely yours,

—M. Perry Bouslog

Five days later, on January 27, 1958, Alphonse wrote the following reply:

My Dear Perry:

We certainly got a kick out of the cartoons enclosed in your letter of January 22. I well remember the incident in Gulfport involving the "Klan" organization meeting. It took a lot of courage for you to be so outspoken at a time when it was popular to "line up."

We are having quite a rough time here with the mail pouring in faster than we can answer it. We had a slight touch of sleet and snow here and on the way up from Raleigh, North Carolina to Petersburg, Virginia; we really had some dangerous driving.

> *I do recall your letter concerning Dwight D. Eisenhower. I note that you will probably be in Brownsville three more months. We have been proudly showing the spear and the shield from your uncle, General Omar Brady's collection which you so kindly gave us. Clatie and Avis join me in sending you warm regards.*
>
>
>
> *Sincerely yours,*
> *Alphonse Lucas,*
> *Secretary*
>
>

"Dad," I said, staring at my father, who was sitting across the table from me. "What does this mean? What did Papa have to do with the Klan?"

"No, Grace, not the Klan," he said, shaking his head. "The Kounter Klan."

"What?"

"It's something people don't talk too much about. A lot of Americans don't want to hear about that period anymore or they want to pretend it didn't exist. But your grandfather, my father, Frank Boykin, started the Kounter Klan—or what was officially known as the Loyalty League, over thirty years before these letters were sent."

"You mean he went to war with the Klan?"

"That's exactly what I mean," Dad smiled.

And, suddenly, it was 1924.

The Ku Klux Klan received legal status to do business in the State of Alabama as a foreign corporation on September 25, 1924.

Frank Boykin stood at a platform, voicing his disapproval to the thousands of Southerners who refused to go along with the Klan's motives and guerilla intimidation tactics.

"We'll start a clan of our own—a Kounter Klan," Boykin pledged. "It will be known as the Loyalty League. Instead of wearing white to show some assumed superiority, we will be cloaked in robes of green, Mother Nature's own color, because we are all her children, regardless of the color of our skin. The members of the Loyalty League will pledge open warfare on the Klan and all its evil purposes."

The crowd roared.

And, still, the fires burned.

This second incarnation of the Klan was the first one to adopt the fiery crosses placed on the front yards of black families. There wasn't quite as much in the way of racial killings, lynching's, or blacks being drawn and quartered, like there was with the early Klan of 1865-1874. But this organization was more insidious, with the KKK platforming for better public schools for poor whites, Prohibition measures, improved road construction, and other seemingly progressive steps to "benefit" society. Their monochromatic version of it, anyway.

Frank Boykin purchased over eight hundred green robes for the Loyalty League's members out of his own pocket, and it was written in his financial ledger under the heading of "Suspense" on November 24, 1924, for $148.65.

The league's members consisted of Catholics, Protestants, Jews, African Americans, and other minorities. It was a polyglot membership, speaking many languages, reflecting the fabric of a growing nation. But unlike the Ku Klux Klan, the Kounter Klan patrolled for the purpose of saving lives, righting wrongs, and protecting the weak and disenfranchised.

As Republican state governments sprouted up, so did the spread of Kounter Klan orders throughout the South, in mostly rural areas. One of Boykin's friends, Congressman Michael McCormack, acknowledged in the congressional records that Frank became president of the "Loyalty League of Alabama, Mississippi, and Louisiana" sector. He organized local Kounter Klan orders that were not centrally controlled but were instead free to act independently—in the same manner of the Ku Klux Klan, yet for very different purposes. It was Frank's version of "fighting fire with fire."

When a Kounter Klan representative learned of Ku Klux Klan actions against black citizens, they would gather local members and raid the KKK meetings, mostly in Mobile, Alabama, disrupting the proceedings and defending the victim.

There were many such skirmishes in Alabama, Mississippi and Louisiana, with the Kounter Klan members banding together to take down the Ku Klux Klan.

"I have information that the Klan will gather in the front yard of a home in Mobile tonight," a Loyalty League member would inform Frank.

"I'll alert our men," was Boykin's response.

In masse, they'd ride their horses at breakneck speed, their green robes fluttering in the wind as they barreled down on the location like an army of uniformed soldiers. There could be nearly a hundred men, but they moved as one with a single mission.

"Stop!" Frank Boykin would shout, as he and the Loyalty League members brought their horses to a halt in front of a roaring flame. Some of the horses reared back, frightened by the large cross burning on the lawn.

Outnumbered and cowardly, the Klan members would disband, scattering as the League put out the last of the fire.

Such confrontations were fraught with violence and danger, but there were others cloaked in robes of social respectability.

Frank told his son Robert the story of those who tried to reincarnate the Ku Klux Klan and lived to regret it. One such individual was Pierre Lafayette; a fearless prosecutor being considered by President Franklin Delano Roosevelt for a possible appointment to the Supreme Court.

Lafayette was charming, seemingly principled and populist. In short, a wolf in sheep's clothing. Though his agenda was based on "reform," it was, in actuality, a front to further causes for white folk and keep the blacks "in their places."

Under sworn examination with the president and his attending staffers, Lafayette vehemently denied the fact that he'd once been a gold card-carrying Klan member. But the truth about Lafayette's character was finally brought to light by a journalist who was a member of Boykin's Kounter Klan. The newspaperman produced a detailed, handwritten list in Lafayette's own writing of the thousand and one corrupt ways in which the politician had hoped to make money, including bribery and extorting bootleggers.

Lafayette tried to bribe the newsman for the evidence, but the journalist was a sworn enemy of the Ku Klux Klan and all they stood for, and would not have any part of Lafayette's generous offer of blood money. Instead, the racist prosecutor was later arrested for the attempted bribe and indicted—all thanks to the integrity of members of the Loyalty League.

Unfortunately, the grand jury itself was filled with Klan members, who forced the prosecution to drop the case for lack of evidence, and in 1926, Lafayette ran for the United States Senate. With the Klan's support, he was elected, although he was taken to task in the press by outraged members of the Kounter Klan.

One of the few defeats Frank Boykin ever knew in his lifetime was seeing Lafayette elected, and it made him that much more determined to protect those who were wronged and to do what was right with his money, brawn, power and contacts. Such determination was what had originally given him the vision and courage to start the Kounter Klan, no matter what it cost him financially or emotionally, and no matter what threats and mental anguish he suffered as a result.

The decision of the Ku Klux Klan to enter politics marked a sinister period in American history. Yet it wouldn't be the last attempt of its kind. Years later, with the appointment of Hugo Black, the Klan would gain some serious headway into U.S. legislation. And Frank Boykin would be in for the fight of his life.

CHAPTER THREE

The Beginning

Frank W. Boykin's story began over one hundred and twenty-four years ago in Bladen Springs, Choctaw County, Alabama. He was one of ten children and held his first job as a water boy to a railroad construction crew at the age of eight. The hard work was an unfortunate necessity. His father died when Frank was still a child, but he immediately found a job to support the rest of his family.

Frank had only two semesters of education and barely learned to read and write but became self-educated through his own efforts and by studying at night with his mother, who was deaf. Before he reached his teens, he was a clerk in a store in Fairford, Alabama, and by the time he was voting age he had his own store and business making crossties for the railroad.

One of his established customers looked at young Frank one day and remarked, "Boykin, what's your secret? For a few years you've been outselling your competitors, who were in the business world a lot longer than you've even been alive!"

As the years went on, Frank harvested a fortune in timber, real estate, livestock and naval stores, as well as investments in land. Like Midas, everything he touched seemed to turn to riches. But he also had a heart of gold. He gained the reputation of being a good Samaritan, as well as a tycoon. Along the way to fame and fortune, he found the time and money to educate his brothers and sisters, picking up the bill for their college educations.

Frank's timber, cattle and farming operations, not to mention his land, have continued through the generations. However, despite his successes in over eighteen various business ventures, he took none of the credit himself, leaving that all to God.

Grace could see the character of the man and his story unfolding before her eyes as she read through the early documents. They said that Frank Boykin was a member of the Methodist Church, a member of the Optimists Club, and was involved with many other charitable organizations. He married a former schoolteacher, Miss Ocllo Gunn of Thomasville, Alabama, and they had five children and thirteen grandchildren together.

"Sounds about right," Grace's father said when she brought up the topic over a dinner of crawdads and crackers. "In fact, my father always gave my mother credit for her help with his letter-writing, her editing and teaching him some of his learning skills."

Grace was happy to hear her father recalling things of his past that he had long forgotten. It was intriguing to hear his recollections, and she began taking notes about his memories of the sessions with Frank Boykin being interviewed by Edward Boykin, who was going to wrote a book of his life titled "Everything Is made for Love" his motto trademarked and book copyrighted in 1973 By Edward Boykin and is out of date.

Before either Grace or her father realized it, though, after hours of interesting talk, the evening had end and they were soon off to sleep. For Grace, however, it was far from a peaceful night's sleep. She dreamt of the past…and the often-nightmarish world of politics.

* * *

The year was 1935. Frank Boykin was already known throughout many states and Washington, especially for his entrepreneurial spirit and the many successful businesses he started.

At that time, the leaders of the Democratic Party and the powers that be in the House started speculating on what sort of man they could find for a successor to fill Judge McDuffie's unexpired term. They knew he would be a Democrat—coming from Alabama, he could not be otherwise. He was also to be a New Dealer.

"We need a relatively new candidate—a student, really—inexperienced in parliamentary procedure, but who will uphold FDR's recovery program," they all agreed.

But, still, questions remained, which the members voiced one by one: "What makes a good congressman? Must he have a college education?" "Must he be a lawyer?" "Should he be a politician?" "Should he have a lot of money in the bank?"

It turned out that Frank Boykin qualified for only one of those things in that he had money. But he literally learned most of what he knew from the school of hard knocks.

Boykin was not a lawyer—but the same would later be true for President Bush, President Regan and President Johnson as well, just to name a few. Instead, the legislators wanted men of business in Congress, which fit Frank to a 'T.'

"So how about this Boykin fellow?" one of the congressmen asked.

"I think he might do," another one answered. "You know his personality—he's filled with an unspeakable energy, love for the people and always seems to have a smile. Those are all qualities and salesman-like skills that can get him re-elected every two years and keep him in the House."

"He's also a huge success in industry and is always ready to go at a minute's notice, which could certainly give him a head start with members who have clout with the administration." Agreeable mutters all around seemed to meet this comment.

"Yes, but he's not a professional politician and has never held political office," came one skeptical voice.

"So? Maybe he's proof that a representative need not be a politician to get elected."

"But the moment he wins the seat—*if* he wins—he'll have to assume the role whether he likes it or not."

With that, the meeting came to an end and the members of the Democratic Committee decided to recruit Frank Boykin as their man.

From the beginning, he was hesitant, resisting until demands from hundreds of people convinced him to drop his reluctance. With the support of his wife and children, Frank finally agreed to run for Congress, hoping to carry on the tradition of many other politicians on Capitol Hill who left a legacy of outstanding service in Alabama.

Accepting the democratic nomination, Boykin vowed, "I am going to cooperate one hundred and ten percent with President Roosevelt and the Democratic leadership in the House." He had even saluted the Supreme Court when it downed the National Recovery Act.

Frank Boykin's campaign to succeed the judge was hailed and a new voice echoed all the way to Capitol Hill. Many of Frank's predecessors took notice as he campaigned against a field of four competitors, which was shortly narrowed down to one. He was like an up-and-coming prize fighter, knocking out his opponents one by one. Yet how he did it was a shock.

"I've got my campaign slogan," Boykin announced to his fellow members of the Democratic Committee one day.

They awaited it anxiously, expecting some take on New Dealism and democracy. Instead, Frank—a strong, distinguished man who, at six feet tall, towered over most people—held up his hands in dramatic fashion to give them the full picture. "Everything's Made for Love," he said.

At first there was silence as the members looked confusedly at one another. Then there was a slight snicker in the assumption—and *hope*—that he had to be kidding.

He wasn't.

"'Everything's Made for Love'?" one member asked incredulously. "What's political about that?"

"What isn't?" Boykin countered. "Behind all great political reform, the main issue is a focus on love. Young or old, everyone should love one's fellow man and their country with no end in sight. As I explained to my son Bob, 'Sooner or later, everyone falls in love.' Therefore, I think 'Everything's Made for Love' is a great campaign slogan. It's what keeps society going."

Suddenly, the stunned silence turned into a silence of awe and admiration for Boykin's obvious sincerity.

"It works for me," one legislator said, echoing the sentiments of the entire group.

Soon, Frank was on the trail day and night, often putting in eighteen-hour days in Mobile and Alabama's First District. He campaigned hard for industrial development, agriculture, the veterans' program, river development, old age, Social Security, education, highways and state integrity. But he never lost sight of his unique slogan, "Everything's Made for Love."

Newspapers were delighted to have a new slogan to publicize—and criticize. To one reporter who was making fun of the slogan, Frank replied, "It means to love one's fellowman, to love life and to love God."

Frank's four-word 'love war cry' echoed among newsmongers around the world, who used the words "motto," "creed," "theme-song," "slogan," "battle cry," "war whoop," and "watchword." It was perhaps the most intriguing campaign slogan employed by an American politician in history. And it was effective.

In 1935, at fifty years of age, Frank Boykin won the congressional election.

Members of the Democratic Committee read the next day's Mobile newspaper, which said, "*Love, though usually considered politically incompatible, is an ancient and honorable emotion.*" Yet it had taken Frank Boykin, a man with no previous political experience, to prove to them all that the old adage that love will find a way still prevailed—even when it came to electing a congressman.

When Frank attended his first White House reception, a smiling President Roosevelt would greet him by saying, "So you're the man who says, 'Everything's Made for Love'?"

"Yes, Mr. President, that's what I believe."

"Well, it looks like you proved it. Keep it going," added FDR as the receiving line moved along.

So, even before he arrived on Capitol Hill, it seemed that Frank Boykin was already aware of—and exuded—the nature and talents it took to become a successful, high-ranking member of Congress.

It was a skill set that would serve him well through the years.

CHAPTER FOUR

House on 'the Hill'

Shortly after winning the election, Frank and his wife had the unenviable task of explaining to their children that they were moving to Washington, D.C. Being a devoted family man, Frank worried about how the kids would take the news—and the reactions were indeed mixed. Naturally, the children didn't want to leave their friends. But they would do anything to support their dad.

Almost immediately upon arrival to their new house in the nation's capital, the Boykin brood was left at the house with their nanny, Martha, when their mother went to see their father being sworn into office. She was anxiously sitting in the House gallery, filled with pride and with a grin from ear to ear, as her husband entered the aisle of the House of Chambers on the arm of his Alabama colleague Lester Hill. Boykin was beaming as he was sworn in as representative from the First District of his beloved state of Alabama. Speaker Joseph Byrnes even stepped down and offered his hand to welcome the newly minted member of the House.

It was a momentous occasion, yet there was much to live up to—and much at stake. Boykin knew this and stated, "Southern leadership was at its pinnacle when I entered Congress on August 12, 1935, and a sensation of excitement dangled over the historic chamber where much of America's destinies were shaped."

At the time of his swearing-in ceremony, the first session of the seventy-fourth Congress was coming to an end with only two weeks left before adjournment. Within this relatively short period of time, almost twenty-five percent of all major legislation passed and was enacted into law.

* * *

Not long after his election, Frank found himself sitting on Capitol Hill alongside notable lawmakers from various states, all of whom would eventually pass into legend. One such member was the chief whip-cracker for the president's majority in the Senate: Joseph T. Robinson of Arkansas. Another was Vice President John Garner of Texas, who currently occupied the platform of the Senate.

Frank was introduced to Vice President Garner shortly after taking his oath, and they instantly became great friends, forming a genuine fondness for one another. Garner gave him the guideline "dos and don'ts" for new members: "Boykin, I have made a few speeches on the floor of either House or I wish I could retract those I have made." (John Garner would retire from the political jungle in 1941. The Boykins would later move into the suite that Garner had occupied at the Washington Hotel.)

Such Southern leaders as Robinson and Garner were some of Roosevelt's greatest supporters and were at the helm of most of the major committees. By the time Boykin took office, however, the 'Nine Old Men' of the Supreme Court had dealt the National Recovery Act (NRA), allowing local codes for fair trade competition to be written by private trade and industrial groups. That was also a big blow to New Dealers.

By declaring *Schechter Poultry Corp. versus United States* unconstitutional, the Court turned it into the famous "chicken case" that invalidated regulations of the poultry industry that were previously circulated under the authority of the NRA in 1933. These regulations included wage fixing, maximum work hours, price of a shipment of chickens (including unhealthy ones) and the right of unions to organize. The ruling was one of a series that overturned elements of President Roosevelt's New Deal legislation. Overnight, the blue eagle symbol of the NRA became a dead fowl whose plucked feathers littered the political arena.

Many legislators, already down over this latest defeat, were initially disappointed when they did not see Frank's theatrical and exuberant personality, which had preceded him to the House, on display at first.

However, as a freshman congressman, Frank conducted himself with tact and observed all the legislative etiquette. He knew to be closed-mouth and defer to the older professionals, which helped him stay clear of the negative trap of inexperience that so many other congressional freshmen fell into.

The making of a congressman is like the making of a baby; it is an aging process. A great and sentimental speaker of the house, Champ Clark of Missouri, once observed, "A member's usefulness should increase in proportion to his length of service. A man has to learn to be a Representative just as a man learns to be a farmer, a lawyer, an engineer, a blacksmith, a carpenter, or a doctor. It was unwise for any district to change Representatives at short intervals. A new Congressman works himself through the channels and committees. Members rise to commanding positions and influence through exercising their brains, tact, energy, courage and industry. Go through the list and there are few exceptions to the rule, that men of long service have the highest places."

An exception to the rule was Frank. Though he was quiet and studious at first, there was another part to his personality. He rose to his toes in an instant, listening and learning the ropes and studying parliamentary procedure. For instance, the quorum (a fixed minimum number of members of the legislature needed to be present in order to conduct business) was a "must," and it was very important to Frank personally. So, he answered the clanging of the quorum bell by going through the corridors of the Capitol and House Office Building with the energy of an aggressive athlete, trying to round up absent members.

Frank wanted to prove to his friends and enemies that what his grandmother had always said was right: that he could do anything to which he applied his God-given talents. He remembered and applied that lesson throughout his life—not least during his first term in the House.

In fact, on only his second day in Congress, Frank anxiously shook hands with four hundred and thirty-four U.S. congressmen, making some instant friends. On Frank's twelfth day after being sworn in, Speaker Byrnes, without any preliminaries, invited him to occupy the chair as speaker-protem and preside over the House deliberations. Many older members of the House and Senate had never had that tribute and were in awe. Some even declared that never in their recollection had a freshman been given such a special honor.

Things were obviously moving fast in Frank's favor.

New and inexperienced congressmen was usually tucked away in a corner on committees that had little to do with shaping the destinies of the republic. Being assigned to big committees was essential and often paved the way for one to climb the seniority ladder. In no time, Frank received such assignments and was placed on three important committees: Merchant Marine and Fisheries, Public Buildings and Grounds, and Patents.

A very desirable suite in the Old House Office Building that would normally go to a senior on the Hill went to Frank. Many veterans on Capitol Hill even preferred it to the gold-plated quarters in the hundred-million-dollar range in the Sam Rayburn Building that was open to lawmakers.

Without delay, Frank's office became Grand Central Station, with a steady stream of constituents and friends from all over the state, and elsewhere, seeking help and guidance from a man with a reputation for great enthusiasm for serving his fellow man.

His office staff, as well as his personal secretary, Alphonse Lucas, all followed him from Mobile. Alphonse was the most astute and loyal co-worker and secretary Frank ever had. He stayed at Frank's right hand and remained loyal to him for forty-seven years in and out of Congress.

In August 1935, Frank moved into the Old House Office Building and his crew instantly went to work decorating the office with historic pictures, guns, knives, a stuffed bear, and other mounted animals that reminded him of his home in Alabama. (After his twenty-eight years of service, it would become a museum of historic memorabilia, telling a story of Frank's life and service to his country.)

Lyndon Johnson was secretary to Congressman Richard Kleberg of Texas, whose office was a few paces down the corridor from Frank's. So, Frank often met Johnson dashing along the hallways.

"Hi, Lyndon," Boykin would call as the young man rushed by.

"Hi, frank," was the response from already down the hall.

The tall, thin, well-spoken young man's agility made a lasting impression on Congressman Boykin, and the Johnsons and Boykins remained on a first-name basis as their friendship developed.

Frank understood that the most important asset of being an effective congressman was to make friends who stood out and had the power to get things accomplished. He busily learned the ropes of the Washington bureaucracy and cultivated the Roosevelt men carrying the ball for the New Deal. In short order, he even earned the right to get close to the man in the White House.

Other congressmen seemed to enjoy and be entertained by Frank's wit, humor, and great stories in the cloakroom. It made him an immediate favorite. With much of the chief House committees having Southerners at the helm as occupying chairmen, the Southern delegation was the most powerful on the Hill. And like all successful Southerners, Frank knew the fine art of tooting his own horn without coming across as a braggart. He succeeded in the House and gained seniority with his unfailing drive and outgoing personality—one catalyst being that he realized he was competing against more than four hundred and thirty other representatives competing for every federal dollar they could get for their respective districts.

When Frank first entered Congress, the main topic of conversation in the Hall on Capitol Hill was the New Deal, as it had been for three years. Franklin Delano Roosevelt was holding control with better than a 75 percent majority in Congress and the Senate. As he addressed his listeners in the media, he'd continually remind them that he possessed a clear-cut mandate from the people to lead the country out of the Great Depression. His message was direct and deliberate about the three R's: rescue, reform and reconstruction.

The New Deal was trudging along with a few of Roosevelt's emergency measures already in place. A lot of discussion was taking place in the cloakrooms about how the recovery measures were subtle and how Congress had complied with the president's demands. Roosevelt's brain, however, was working overtime in trying to get his ideas implemented for the remedy of the nation's economic woes.

Boykin entered Congress after the passage of the Wagner Act—Labor's so-called 'Magna Carta.' Through this, the New Deal was doling out only a meager share of federal relief and emergency spending money to Alabama. In fact, fewer New Deal funds were being channeled to

Alabama's First District than to any other congressional district in the United States.

That didn't sit well with one new member.

Frank kept his district of Alabama foremost in his mind. He fought on the battlefront for his constituents and capitalized on whatever he could for their benefit. He realized the neglect that his home state was undergoing at the hands of the federal government, which was without parallel in the whole history of the nation. That only caused him to fight harder to make good on his campaign promises to get everything within reach for his district. Soon, his effectiveness and ambition to get federal funds were heard and felt throughout Alabama.

Most statesmen on Capitol Hill began hurrying home on August 26, when Congress adjourned. They would spend their time repairing political fences and

enjoying their families. But Frank remained close to the money and was the only member of the Alabama delegation to make the sacrifice. During the vacation recess, he stood by his guns and worked as much as eighteen hours a day on his district's behalf. Unlike the rest, Congressman Boykin's office never closed; it operated seven days a week. At a difficult time, Frank even took money from his own pocket to pay for the extra help he had to hire in order to answer his mail, which was more than that of anyone else in Congress. But Frank made sure that no letter went unanswered. (Speaker William B. Bankhead once offered a simple answer to the secret of getting re-elected term after term: "Give close and prompt attention to your mail. Your votes and speeches in the House may make you well known and give you a reputation, but it is the way you handle your mail that determines your re-election.")

With his inexhaustible energy, Frank walked the halls on behalf of department heads in charge of purse-strings for the New Deal. Having traveled throughout Washington and the halls of the Hill on just such a mission, he inspired one columnist to write:

> *Alabama's new congressman, Frank Boykin, is literally setting the woods afire around Washington in pursuit of money projects for Alabama. His unusual energy is greatly admired by many who are weary of attempting to get proper consideration*

of the claims of their Districts. The Alabama Congressman apparently never tires. He is always on the go all the time. If the First District of Alabama does not get its share, it will not be because Congressman Boykin has not presented the claims of his District to everybody in the national capital.

Frank personally carried his pleas for funds for Alabama directly to Franklin D. Roosevelt—and it was not too surprising that FDR succumbed to the impact of the Boykin charm.

One day after an eloquent plea from Frank, the president's eyes began twinkling. "Frank," he said, "one of these days you'll come down and ask me to move the Treasury Building to Alabama."

"No, Mr. President," Frank replied. "Just move the money down to Alabama and that'll be sufficient."

CHAPTER FIVE

The 'Hunt' for Federal Funds

In December 1935, Frank delivered a graphic display to promote the welfare of his district. He hosted an unusual hunting party on his large game preserve in McIntosh, Alabama. Not every man possesses a game preserve, but since he owned one anyway, Frank saw no valid reason not to capitalize on it by using it to improve his district's fortune.

He invited many players in Washington, outstanding political figures from around the nation, as well as those who held administrative positions and had the authority to say yes or no to spending federal money in Alabama or any other state in the Union. His purpose, he explained, was "to show these men the undeveloped possibilities of Alabama for Federal appropriations and who will be glad to help us when Congress convenes." It was an expensive and elaborate gesture that eventually captured for him the title of the "greatest party-giver in the history of Congress."

It was a rare combination for a politician to be a salesman and a showman. But Frank was both. The expedition personally cost him more than a year's salary to show off his district, but he couldn't have been prouder to do it.

This was the scene that greeted the Washington elite: arriving in Mobile, Frank escorted his many guests on a tour of the city, which was blooming beautifully with azaleas. After that came a cruise down the fabled Mobile Bay. Then it was off to his game preserve, surrounding the beautiful antebellum plantation home that was first built in 1905 for the Agnes Miles family. The thousands of acres of pristine hunting grounds

Ten days later, Snader and his wife met Frank in Mobile. They paraded past the sights and wonders of the Tombigbee and the towns along its banks, pausing at several charming small communities. The next day, they went up to Montgomery, where Governor Graves gave them the royal treatment. They dined on a fine Alabama fried chicken dinner.

Shortly afterward, Vanity Fair announced the removal of its first mill from Monroeville, Pennsylvania, which continued with the company pulling up most of its stakes from that state and moving their plants to Alabama. The thriving business, which operated all over the world, opened plants in Monroeville, Jackson, Demopolis and Atmore, Alabama, and there were thousands of happy locals on their payrolls.

For a long time, Frank, pleased with this success, made a practice of sending nightgowns and other feminine delights made by Vanity Fair to the wives of the presidents. When he and his wife, Ocllo, were going down the receiving line at the White House, Mrs. Eisenhower repeated her thanks for the hostess gown he had sent her, saying, "I think of you every time I put it on."

The president smiled and added, "She puts it on several times a day."

CHAPTER SEVEN

"Kings" of the Hill

President Roosevelt had caught Congress off-guard, first with the wage-hour fight and then by nominating Senator Hugo Black to the Supreme Court. Black's confirmation as an associate justice promised a royal battle in the Senate. Liberals were pleased; conservatives went into spasms of discontentment.

Black's record and life were open to utmost scrutiny. His previous affiliations as a card-carrying Ku Klux Klan devotee were aired across the nation. Congress, however, held him with a mixture of approval and denunciation. In the cloakrooms, the gossip was that were Black not a senator, he would not have received five votes. Yet with all the predictions of senatorial disapproval, Black was still confirmed...with a few frowns to be found on some Congressional faces—among them Frank's.

Frank would draw the comparison of Black to Pierre Lafayette, who tried to reincarnate the Ku Klux Klan and increase its power through political position. Frank and many others were disheartened to have Black succeed to the Supreme Court, wondering how he made it through the process having been a Ku Klux Klan member.

Despite the opposition, on October 4, 1937, Black donned the judicial robe. Governor Grave appointed his wife, Dixie, as interim senator from Alabama and ordered a special election in April to choose Black's successor. Representative Lister Hill would win the Senate seat vacated by Black.

A dissident group calling itself Independent Young Americans blasted Black with a full-page headline that read: "Black Day" and many everything. I am ready to reciprocate now or at any other time," which sounded politically awful.

Editors, Drew Pearson and other members of the press seized the opportunity to write about this supposed infraction. Even Frank's hometown paper charged him with favoring the Alabama Power Company over the development of the "people's very own" TVA.

Because of the negative publicity, Frank lost the committee seat to Representative Philip Ferguson of Oklahoma by a single vote. However, on May 5, the First District re-elected Frank to Congress in a three-to-one majority. (In January 1939, Frank would be appointed as a member of the Rivers and Harbors Committee. In May of 1940, veteran representative J.J. Mansfield of Oklahoma, chairman of the Rivers and Harbors Committee, would write to Frank: *"This Congress is coming to a close and I cannot let this opportunity go by without thanking you for the valuable aid you rendered in the long and tedious work; the broad outlook you have on national problems and the harmonizing effect of your buoyant disposition make your services as a working member of the committee of the highest value."*

Personal accolades did not come as easily for Frank's friend Senator Walter George of Georgia. President Roosevelt claimed that he crippled the court-packing and other New Deal measures, and named Walter as the principal target for defeat in the 1938 primaries, wanting to oust the veteran from the Senate. The people turned a deaf ear to FDR's plea and returned George to his seat by an overwhelming majority.

The morning after the primaries, Frank sent this congratulatory telegram to George:

> *Well, Walter you won a great victory against insurmountable odds. Georgia, the South and the entire nation are thankful and happy. Now we know that with you in the great United States Senate for another six years you will as in the past safely guard all the people's rights. All Alabama and the rest of the nation sat up last night praying for George in Georgia, and at last the glad tidings came joyfully through music on the radio at 8:00 A.M.... To me and mine it seemed as though the message came direct from Heaven, and maybe it did, but it was also direct from thinking men and women of Georgia in our Southland.*

While this is your great personal victory it is also a victory for true Democracy. We have already thanked the Good Lord for giving you to us again, and I want to thank those great loyal Democrats in Georgia. God bless you and give you strength to carry on.

The victories, however, were far from over.

On a June day, Frank and Representative Jasper Bell of Missouri had time for a rare lunch in the crowded House restaurant. Hardly were they seated before a well-dressed black man, accompanied by two elegantly attired white women and several white men, entered and asked to be served. They were representing the Greater New York Industrial Council, which had spent the morning demonstrating in the Capitol corridors because seventeen Democrats of the House from New York had absented themselves when the House overrode President Roosevelt's veto of the no-strike bill.

Capitol police had been alerted to the disturbance before it even took place, and the head waiter explained to the group that the restaurant was reserved exclusively for members of the House and their guests. The black man protested loudly. Charging racial discrimination, he noisily asserted that he was an American citizen, and as such was entitled to dine in the House restaurant, just as any member of Congress. The head waiter replied that no one, white or black, was permitted to eat in the restaurant unless they were guests of a congressman.

Overhearing the disturbance, Speaker Will Bankhead, who was lunching nearby, rose and stepped over to Frank's table. "Frank," he said, "I wish you'd go over and get that crowd out of here."

"Mr. Speaker," replied Frank, "I'll be glad to do it, if you'll promise to keep out of the way. There may be a fight."

With little disturbance, Frank managed to persuade them to come outside, where he resolved the matter peaceably.

Shortly after that resolution, Frank found that he had a much larger success on his hands. On July 13, 1939, Secretary of War Woodring announced the selection of the city for the site of the Air Force's new Southern Depot, which would be a vital component of America's defense. It was to be constructed in Mobile's harbor—at a cost of eight million dollars—and would be called Brookley Field Air Force Base, named for the brilliant aviator Captain William Brookley of Nebraska, who was killed at Bolling Field in an airplane crash in 1934. (Tampa, Florida, was picked as the commanding installation station.)

The government ended up building a $26.5-million facility for aircraft modification and a supply depot with access to Mobile. Shipbuilding boomed as a result of the demand for supplies. At the same time, because Mobile had sent so many young men to war, employment demands were difficult to meet. African Americans and women were presented with jobs that had never existed before. There were as many as sixteen thousand workers employed on the base at one time.

On March 19, 1941, Uncle Sam took possession of over one thousand acres of land adjacent to Mobile in order to construct air depot. *"That means,"* wrote a Mobile paper, *"that Uncle Sam turned loose nine hundred forty thousand dollars at once for construction. When he has finished the depot the staff payroll will be a minimum of one million two hundred thousand dollars a year. It is expected that the Mobile base would eventually be the largest of the Air Force's Depots, and the only one on tidewater."*

Fast-forward to 1962, and the government's investment in the Brookley base will have reached a billion dollars, with a yearly payroll of over one hundred million.

Thrilled with his state's good fortune, Frank was quoted as saying, "As long as I am in office, you'll have Brookley Field."

However, years later, as soon as Frank left office, it wouldn't take long for the base—which was Mobile's largest employer, with an annual salary payout of $95 million—to be closed by the Department of Defense.

Lesson learned: You can't win them all. But if Frank was in office, he was determined to do just that.

CHAPTER EIGHT

The Telegram That Changed History

Early in the morning of August 1940, Frank boarded a taxi at the Capitol and sped to the White House. After hurriedly revealing his mission to presidential secretary Marvin McIntyre, he was immediately ushered into FDR's private office, where the president read the telegram that Frank hastily handed to him.[1]

"Frank," he said, "I want you to see Lord Lothian, the British Ambassador, at once and have him read this telegram. Tell him exactly what you've just told me. This information is too valuable to keep away from the British. Say nothing to anyone about this."

Leaving the White House in a rush, Frank taxied to the British Embassy, where he presented the telegram to Lord Lothian, who was impressed at its detail. He promptly communicated it to London by transatlantic telephone.

What the telegram contained would change the course of history.

* * *

Earlier that day, the Boykins had risen, as usual, with the firing of the cannon at Fort Myer across the Potomac. Ocllo was reading aloud from their hometown newspaper, the *Mobile Press Register*, when her eyes lit upon a column titled "A Hundred Years Ago Today," which told the story of a group of intrepid Alabamians who, a century before, had built a

---

[1] The following was taken from the book *Everything's Made for Love* by Edward Boykin (p. 99-102).

dam at McGrew's Shoals on the Tombigbee River near Jackson, Alabama. While drilling and blasting for the dam's foundation, they struck a strong stream of oil that, within several days, had coated the surface of the river as far down as Fort Stoddert, sixty miles below the shoals.

A party of Indians set the oil afire. Flames engulfed the river, which burned like an inferno for miles and miles. Blazing oil enveloped the swamps along the riverbank, cremating hundreds of deer, bear and small game. Turkeys, quail and owls fleeing the holocaust were de-feathered or destroyed. Thousands of trees, fine timber along the river's edge, were burned to ashes. People traveled miles to gaze in silent awe at the broad, burning river that, for three days, had devoured everything within reach.

"Frank," said Ocllo, glancing up from her reading, "this thing has given me an idea."

"I'll bet it's the same as mine," replied Frank. "And I'm going to do something about it right now."

Husband and wife had gotten the same idea at the same exact moment. They had earlier been talking about England's plight and wondering, as was the whole world, just when Hitler would invade that country. "Why," they seemed to ask each other silently, "couldn't the British set the English Channel afire—just as the Tombigbee was set afire a century ago—and destroy the German invasion fleet and barges loaded with troops, tanks and guns?"

It was just 5:00 a.m., but Frank called his close friend, Joe Danziger, who lived in Fort Worth, Texas. Joe had known oil all his life, and when he answered the phone, Frank immediately asked him if the idea was feasible. He listened alertly to what Frank said and gave an emphatic, "Yes."

Two hours later, Frank had a five-hundred-word telegram from his friend explaining exactly what to do. It would require dumping enormous quantities of oil on the Channel waters and setting it afire with bullets and flares. This was the telegram Frank showed to both President Roosevelt and Lord Lothian.

At that dark hour in Britain's history, Winston Churchill, with eloquence that would resound through the ages, had assumed the position of prime minister and rallied his people. Months before, in May of 1940, Adolph Hitler had unleashed his long-anticipated Western offensive. His divisions blazed through the Low Countries and overtook France's line. Denmark and Norway had fallen prey to the Nazi party.

It was in the air over the "English isles" that Hitler had paused at the Channel, his panzers panting for more work to do, a million of his Wehrmacht poised to resume their bombardment. Hitler's Operation Sea Lion, an invasion of England, was target dated for late September. Meanwhile, Britain got ready. Residents and visitors were urged to curtail seashore outings. Church bells were silenced and ordered to ring only to warn of parachutist invasion. The little island mobilized to meet the Nazi onslaught on her soil.

By the end of June, Hitler's swastika flew over Europe from the Pyrenees to the North Cape of Norway. England was on the verge of absolute, unconditional defeat. There was talk of bargaining with Hitler, of handing over the British fleet before he crossed the Channel and erased what the world had once known as "England."

On September 7, the Luftwaffe, bombers and fighters, roared through the late afternoon towards England. Target: London. For fifty-six nights, wave on wave, Hitler's vultures discharged death and destruction on the great metropolis of the world. This was the Blitz, Hitler's next-to-last card in the Battle of Britain if his bombers could break the spirit and pride of the British people by raining sorrow, misery and fire from the night skies, devastating London itself if need be. They would force the Churchill government to capitulate and ask for terms, after thousands of the Wehrmacht were transported across the Channel to complete the conquest of the British Isles.

It was not to be.

Many believe that Hitler's greatest mistake was the failure to invade Britain in September of 1940, when she appeared defenseless and bombers could cause the destruction of her proudest city. Instead, on September 16, 1940, the Royal Air Force met Hitler's invasion fleet in the Channel and destroyed it.

In exterminating Hitler's seaborne army, the RAF used the technique suggested by oil man Joe Danziger, which had been relayed to the British through Frank Boykin via President Roosevelt and, in turn, Lord Lothian. RAF bombers covered the waters of the Channel with oil, igniting it with flares and combustible bullets. The invasion armada was enveloped in a sea of flames that incinerated or injured an estimated fifty thousand German soldiers. It also destroyed the invasion fleet, crowded with troops, artillery, tanks and material.

Several times toward the end of 1944, President Roosevelt brought up the subject with Frank, simply saying, "Frank, I think you ought to know your idea was used. It served its purpose amply."

Later, Frank revealed, "Lord Lothian told me in confidence that the idea had been carried out by the British and that an attempted invasion of England by the Germans was thwarted through its use."

* * *

In 1943, the full story of Hitler's invasion was brought to light. Datelined in London, the story appeared under the by-line of a United Press correspondent. He pieced it together from what he learned from Belgian nurses and doctors who had cared for survivors of the Holocaust, and by intimate contact with higher-ups of the exiled government in London.

"I was told in Antwerp," said this correspondent, "that the Germans had concentrated hundreds of self-propelled barges, each about one hundred and sixty feet long that had been used on the Rhine and continental rivers. Belgian nurses told me that the German survivors had called Hitler's battle 'a hellish nightmare.' Belgians with whom I talked were surprised to learn that the British and American public had never been told of the failure of the invasion attempt. It was common knowledge in Belgium.

"Renee Meurisse, a Belgium Red Cross nurse, oversaw the caring for Belgium refugees at the time; she said, 'During the day of September 17, we heard rumors that thousands of bodies of German soldiers were being washed ashore along the Belgian beaches. That night at 7:00 P.M., a German Red Cross train of forty coaches pulled into the Brussels station. We had been expecting a Belgian refugee train and were surprised when it was filled with Germans. A German officer, who looked tired, approached me and asked if we could give aid to his wounded.' Miss Meurisse said the German officer told her his train had been on the wrong line and 'my men are dying from lack of treatment.' 'We sent a call for more nurses and ambulances and began taking the wounded from the train,' she said. 'The moans and screams were terrible.'

"'I helped carry one young German soldier from the train to the stretcher. He was horribly burned about the head and shoulders. The doctor and I placed this soldier in a corner, and we decided we could find out what happened. We began by asking him about his mother and then about his sweetheart. After each answer I asked him: where were you going when this happened?

"'Finally, we pieced together the whole story. He said they had been told they were going to invade Britain, that nothing could stop them and that it was just a matter of getting into the boats and going across the Channel.

"'He said, "It was horrible. The whole Channel was in flames. The British bombed and machine-gunned us. Hell couldn't be worse."

"'And then he died on the stretcher.'

"'We cared for more than five hundred soldiers. Many of them died there in the Brussels station.'"

* * *

Those intrepid dam-builders at McGrew's Shoals on the Tombigbee River over a century before would have never dreamed that they would set the pattern for a future generation to save the world from the Nazis.

In a letter to the *Mobile Press Register* in 1944, Frank's partner, Joe Danziger, wrote of the idea that thwarted the Nazi invasion of England. *"It is Frank and his alertness that all credit is due in grasping the importance of ideas suggested to him and acting upon them immediately. The State of Alabama can well be proud of your great Congressman and our only regret is that he does not hail from Texas."*

CHAPTER NINE

Upheavals of the 1940s

As Bob Boykin read through the letters with Grace, he remembered his father telling him about the large luncheon he hosted, inviting many of his colleagues to the Speaker's Dining Room in the Capitol. Fireworks exploded in the room. Frank had with him one hundred thousand "Bankhead for President" buttons and pinned them on everybody he could as they were entering. He even sent one to the president, who scribbled off a note of thanks: "Dear Frank, you always were an early bird. I hope you're not too early this time," wrote FDR.

The Deep South echoed with Speaker Will Bankhead's cry for presidential nomination at the Democratic Convention in June. Frank topped off his Bankhead-for-President boom with this statement: "A Bankhead in the White House would mean a great deal to Alabama. If we don't get Will Bankhead in the White House, maybe we can maneuver around to make him vice president. However, I believe he would make one of our greatest presidents."

That wasn't the only election on the horizon. May was coming up fast—time for the primaries to determine Frank's re-election. He had four opponents running against him. In an appeal to the First District voters, he said, "I believe my record deserves at least one trip to Washington without opposition. I can do better for Mobile and this district if I am not hampered by the necessity of conducting a campaign. My part in bringing new industries here in promoting the Air Depot, and aiding Alabama businessmen, foresters, and farmers is known to most and should deserve a recognition that would allow me to continue in this work without the burden of a campaign. However, I am not worried about winning elections now; I am chiefly concerned with building up Alabama."

The voters of the First District wholeheartedly agreed and sent him back to Congress with a three-to-one victory.

The National Democratic Convention in Chicago in July had some fireworks but looked to be a clear-cut success for Franklin D. Roosevelt. Frank, however, had the job of helping to nominate the convention's keynoter, Will Bankhead, for whom he was prepared to whoop it up until the cows came home—quite literally. He ransacked Chicago for cowbells to help with the Bankhead demonstration!

The cards were stacked against Will Bankhead, who received 329 votes on the first ballot for presidential nominee. After that, it was a shoo-in for FDR, who took Henry Wallace as his vice president.

Two months later, on September 15, 1940, Will Bankhead have died and Frank lost a great friend.

Sam Rayburn from Bonham, Texas, was the second man in the history of the government to win the high post of majority leader without a contest. The only other one to do it was the deceased Speaker, William Bankhead, whom Rayburn succeeded.

Rayburn accepted the presiding officer's gavel "in great humility." He was the second Texan to ascend to the great office and was also a wonderful friend of Frank's. He had escalated to the highest post in the House, and his promotion to the third-highest role in the nation only seemed to make them closer friends.

* * *

Though the Bankhead nomination didn't go as hoped, that was just the beginning of the turbulent '40s for Frank. First, he had the honor of driving in one of the large bolts that held the steel plates together when they laid the keel of the massive battleship *Alabama* at her honoring and last anchorage in Mobile waters. He wrote to Governor Dixon, "All Alabama will be proud of this mighty ship that will go on and on, and so many people all over the earth will know about Alabama, who do not know, for truly it is the greatest State in the Union. Our state will have an advertisement that will go on and on." In February 1941, the ship was launched at Norfolk, Virginia; Frank was there, glorying in the great day.

his fire at each member of the Alabama House delegation. The best, or rather the worst, he could say about Frank Boykin was that he was "one of the best lumberjacks in his neck of the woods." He then warned that the voters would take revenge at the upcoming election time. But they upheld the anti-strike bill, and the idea of 'revenge' failed to catch on with the voters. In 1942, for the first time, Frank was unopposed for re-election.

Frank also vehemently supported the Civilian Conservation Corps (CCC). As news reporter Drew Pearson recounted in his headline story, "Mobile's Bass Drum Congressman": "Frank is a warm supporter of conservation and forestry, which he practiced on his vast lands in Alabama. He wanted the Civilian Conservation Corps (CCC) as a permanent agency of the government. It was the fundamental soundness of the New Deal creation that he crusaded in thirty States to keep on the government's agenda."

Frank said, "I have always been a great admirer and booster of the CCC and was in the thick of the fight when this agency was threatened with drastic curtailment of another agency. The work done by the CCC in the rehabilitation of young men, in the conservation of our forests and soil, in praise of men and women in all walks of life and in all political parties. I am heartily in favor of making the Civilian Conservation Corps a permanent Federal agency."

Then, on December 7, 1941, came the "day that will live in infamy," as a devastating war was hurled across the Pacific. As Edward Boykin wrote in *Everything Is Made for Love*, "Mobile became a bustling center of war activity. Her shipyards were soon working round the clock, building huge cargo and tank ships. War workers flooded into the city and the combining population soared to one hundred and thirty-five thousand."

How did that happen? Frank had summoned officials of various Southern shipyards to Washington, where he led them—as well as Alabama's entire congressional delegation—before the Maritime Commission to urge that shipbuilding contracts be given to Southern shipyards. Admiral Vickery, right then and there, turned down their request, observing in so many words that the South possessed neither the brains nor the abilities to build ships for the United States. Vickery even ventured to state that only over his "dead body" would the South be given contracts by the commission.

Frank replied with words that ripped and burned. He closed his attack with the statement that the South could not only build ships cheaper than the North but infinitely better. Yet the outlook for Southern shipyards looked bleak. The commission was unchangeable. Even Senator John Bankhead told Frank he was butting his head against a stone wall and would be better off to forget it.

Bullheaded as ever, Frank—a member of the House Merchant Marines and Fisheries Commission that appropriated the money for the Maritime Commission to build ships—found a way to bring the Maritime Commission in line. A West Coast congressman from California was likewise outraged by the commission's cold-shouldering of the shipyards in his state, and he threw his chips in with Frank, who got enough votes in the committee to block the commission's appropriation to build ships anywhere! He then went to see Vickery.

"If you don't give the South and the West Coast a fair share of your shipbuilding contracts," he told them, "I'll see that not a dollar is voted for the commission to do anything."

"But you can't do that," flared Vickery.

"The hell I can't!" blazed Frank. "I can and I will. And it will be over *your* dead body, if you like it. I have the votes to do just what I've said."

"All right," said Chairman Bland. "We'll give ship contracts to the Southern builders, but we won't pay your workers the same wage we pay to Northern shipyard workers. Southern workers don't need that much money to live on."

"You'll do no such thing!" said Frank. "You'll pay the same wage scale to Southern workers that you pay to those in the North."

Bland and Vickery capitulated unconditionally. Within days, Southern shipbuilders were flooded with billions of dollars in ship contracts and Mobile became a madhouse of activity.

However, the Maritime Commission canceled Andrew Jackson Higgins' sixty-five-million-dollar contract to construct a shipyard in Mobile and build two hundred Liberty ships. In this case, the commission was told there was a shortage of steel. Later, Higgins was appointed chairman of a special House Merchant Marine Committee to examine why and what the actuality of the steel shortage was, while in the upper chamber, Senator Harry Truman launched a similar inquiry.

The Boykin Committee also dug deep, finally turning in a report that laid the blame for the shortage that existed on the bungling of the War Production Board. There was no actual shortage of steel. It was like sugar, who's supposed shortage was publicized into an alarming condition that irritated housewives for the duration of the war, only to wind up with warehouses bulging with the sweet staple. Even carbonated beverage companies like Barg were, in 1941, having problems getting sugar and kept begging for more for several years. (Is sounds and appears as though the same thing could be going on today with the oil and gas 'shortages and rising prices. Is history repeating itself?)

The Boykin Committee was the first to unmask the War Production Board's tragic mishandling of war material production and forced the arrogant agency to rescind many of their rulings. Millions of housekeepers gave a rousing "thank goodness" when the WPB announced that bakeries would be permitted to resume slicing bread for home consumption. In the same breath, it disowned its brainchild that had produced a shortage of diapers and put the agency on what a commentator called "the spot and a very wet, uncomfortable spot," indeed!

In January 1943, a new honor was conferred on Frank with his appointment as chairman of the House Patents Committee, a task he welcomed, knowing that hundreds of the nation's most valuable patents were being handed over to the wrong Allies. He was well-versed in patents, as he had several of his own with his turpentine business, and so Chairman Boykin sponsored and steered through the legislative mill for a bill to clarify the patent laws.

The United States Patent system was the best in the world and the committee was determined to keep it that way. During the hearings on this measure, it was testified before the committee that Vice President Henry Wallace, while serving as secretary of commerce, had handed over to Soviet Russia over six thousand American patents. When Wallace was called before the committee to explain his actions, he readily admitted what he had done and said, "Why, the Russians were our allies, weren't they?" He also voiced admiration for the Soviet Union and their policies of central planning for the welfare of the working classes.

The Boykin Patent Act, finally voted into law, was often cited as "one of the most constructive pieces of legislation affecting patents enacted by Congress in a single generation."

* * *

Talk on Capitol Hill of organizing into a new party of displeased Democrats and the anti-Southern delegation of the New Deal inspired Frank to proclaim he was not actually against the New Deal, which, overall, had been "pretty good" to the South. "There's a whole lot of talk about a new party. Frank preferred to keep the good old party. Keep it right and clean and fine but get rid of the Communists and crackpots in the Democratic ranks." The chief object of this verbal assault was Henry Wallace, who might have become president of the United States.

The House was in a bitter fight over the Connally-Harkness Antistrike Bill, which became a target of every missile in the New Deal and Labor arsenal. This measure was designed to outlaw a strike in war industries. It was a simple act of old-fashioned patriotism. The New Deal "assassins" ordered a "must kill" that backfired on the killers. The bill was enacted into law, with 101 Democrats and 118 Republicans voting for it; Frank was a strong supporter of the bill. On the heels of this New Deal defeat, the American Federation of Labor published what it designated a "Roll Call of Labor's Enemies." In an unconvincing message, President Roosevelt vetoed the bill, but Congress responded by overriding his veto with swiftness. Not surprisingly, the talks of the Hill and of the American people in the spring of 1944 was the political question, "Would Franklin D. Roosevelt run for a fourth term?"

There was a "Sam Rayburn for vice president" rivalry forming in the House as the Southern bloc announced its intention of opposing the re-nomination of Vice President Henry Wallace. Wallace, as secretary of agriculture, sentenced six million little pigs to death in 1933. Texan Lyndon B. Johnson was the only one of the twenty-five Southern members of the House polled on the "stop Wallace movement" who expressed doubt of Rayburn's chances of landing second place on the Democratic ticket. Johnson declared, "You can't eliminate the fact that the President is going to select the Vice President."

At the 1944 National Democratic Convention was thought that FDR could continue to occupy the White House for the rest of his life, if he so desired. He ran his own New Deal railroad to suit himself. He was engineer, fireman, brakeman; he threw all the switches, waved all the flags. But the big question was: Who would Roosevelt choose for vice presidency?

Behind the scenes of the Chicago convention, Frank was resolved to block Wallace's re-nomination, stating, "I like a good fight, especially when the things you are fighting for mean preservation of our democratic way of life and the salvation of our great national freedoms, which have been traditional among the people of the South for generations. I want to see John Bankhead nominated for the vice president, though I know he would be willing to bow to the will of the majority should the Southern delegates consolidate to as a group to support some other candidate."

Former Senator James Byrnes of South Carolina was the unofficially agreed-on nominee for vice president by many of the Southern delegates. When Frank reached Chicago in July of that year, he went at once to see Senator Byrnes in his suite at the Stevens Hotel. His wife was with him. They had chatted for about fifteen minutes when the phone rang with a call from President Roosevelt in Yuma, Arizona.

Byrnes listened to the one-sided conversation with Roosevelt, taking notes in shorthand. Ten minutes later, he said, "But, Mr. President, I don't care to clear it with Sidney, as you suggest." As he hung up the phone, he turned to Frank: "Wallace is to be vice president. FDR says I am not acceptable to Sidney Hillman or to Labor and that Wallace must be the nominee." Frank assured Byrnes, "As long as I have a breath in my body, I will fight Wallace's re-nomination."

Byrnes informed Frank that he felt the only man who could head off Wallace was Senator Harry Truman of Missouri, with which Frank agreed. On leaving Byrnes, Frank phoned John Bankhead to find the senator had weakened his candidacy. Undeterred, Frank moved on with his exuberance, calling Senator Scott Lucas of Illinois, who had the powerful backing of Chicago's Mayor Kelly. Lucas insisted there wasn't a chance of heading off Wallace, but Frank countered by offering a trade: if, on the first ballot, Lucas received more votes than Bankhead, Senator Bankhead would throw his strength to Lucas; if the opposite happened, Lucas would toss his backing to Bankhead. Convinced he had nothing to lose, Lucas accepted the proposed swap.

A variety of dark horses and favorite sons were stomping around the convention: Alben Barkley of Kentucky, Senator O'Mahoney of Wyoming, Sam Rayburn of Texas, and Harry Truman of Missouri. On the convention's first ballot, Wallace polled 429 votes; Truman, 319; and Bankhead, 98. Having snared fewer votes than Bankhead, Lucas informed Frank that the trade would be honored the moment Frank called for it.

The second ballot brought little change from the first. In the interim between second and third ballots, Senator Bankhead, at Frank's urging by phone from the convention floor, announced the release of his twenty-four delegates to Truman. Next, Frank called Lucas to release his delegates to Bankhead and, in turn, to Truman.

Alabama's bolt to Truman swept the rest of the Southern states along with it. It was this turnaround that sparked the momentum to hurl Harry Truman onto the vice presidential nominee and into the presidency.

* * *

Shortly after the 1944 Democratic convention turned thumbs-down on his re-nomination, ex-vice president Henry Wallace embarked on a tour of Europe. He sweet-talked the Russians and called many Americans "imperialists and fascists." He also referred to capitalists as "midget Hitlers," and publicly criticized Truman's "get rough" policy towards the Soviet Union. Frank was so outraged at these attacks on his country that he cabled former premier Winston Churchill, assuring him that Wallace did not speak for America, the American people, or the government, and that he holds no public office.

In a follow-up letter, Frank bluntly denounced Wallace's conduct:

> *"I was amazed that an American, who had held such a high position in our government, would even think of going to foreign countries and try to tear down what our great leaders were trying to do.*
>
> *"Our people, many of them are much upset about Mr. Wallace. I have heard many men in high offices say he should*

be put into an institution. Some say the President should revoke his passport, when he reaches Russia, and leave him there where he belongs. I don't believe the man knows what he is doing. I want the people in England and all over Europe to know that this man, who is considered by many as a crackpot, was not speaking for this great government.

"It seems to me that it is the same old racket, divide and destroy, and it seems he is trying to divide or separate Great Britain and the United States. I think when your people voted your party out and put the other party in, that came nearest separating us than anything that has ever happened, and if they didn't then nothing will.

"We are having our troubles but will work them out. Our fine people are getting back on their feet. Our boys are becoming acclimated. They have been all over the earth, fighting on land and sea and air, and they are bound to be disturbed, and it is only natural that it takes time for them to become normal and get back into a routine, but they are coming, and with the leadership of this great Truman, we are bound to settle down and start producing. Our laboring people are the finest folk in the world. We have a few racketeers, and this is our only trouble. You have then everywhere, not only in labor, but in every business.

"We are praying that God will give you strength to carry on for your country and the entire World."

Churchill's Honorary Secretary Edmond D.A. Odd replied to Frank in a personal letter on June 6, 1947:

Dear Sir,
On behalf of Mr. Churchill, I am writing to thank you for your letter of 28th May 1947.
I am afraid Mr. Churchill has given all his photographs away because, as you can imagine, there has been a pretty large call on them in the last few years.

With reference to your question regarding reactions to Mr. Wallace over here, you will have seen from the papers that Mr. Churchill commented on Mr. Wallace's behavior in a speech he made while Mr. Wallace was here, and I don't think he has any further comments to make.

Yours faithfully,
Edmond D.A. Odd

On June 18, 1947, Elizabeth Elliott, the private secretary to Winston Churchill, wrote the following to Frank:

Dear Sir,
I am so sorry that no reply has been sent earlier to your letter to Mr. Churchill of the 13th of May.
Mr. Churchill thanks you very much for your letter; he read this with interest, and the enclosures in it. He does not feel able, however, to make the comments for which you ask, as the pressure of his work is so great. In this he hopes you will understand and excuse him.

Yours truly,
Elizabeth Elliott

Apparently, there was a mix-up in Churchill's office among the secretaries since Frank received a letter from both acknowledging the same letter he had written. However, Churchill also responded promptly to Frank's urgings by broadcasting a warning to the British people not to be taken in by Wallace's smears.

Frank received the following letter dated May 3, 1947, from Harris Brothers Ranch, Los Angeles, Texas (La Salle County):

Dear Frank:
The recent talks of Henry Wallace in Europe, criticizing the foreign policy of our American Government, bring to the minds of many how kind providence was to our people that Wallace today is not president. Yet you and I know only too

well how close this disaster came to striking our nation and the world.

Frank, here I am in my native state of Texas, less than a mile from where I was born, and I have had little time to reflect upon the historical happenings at the 1944 Democratic Convention in Chicago. What a lasting debt of gratitude our people owe you, our friend, the late Senator John Bankhead, many other southern leaders, and Chairman Robert Hannegan, for blocking Wallace's nomination at the 1944 Convention.

I can never forget the day of July 20, 1944, when you, and your co-patriots, succeeded in preventing Wallace's nomination as was scheduled for that day. Especially after the convention adjourned, and the midnight meeting in my room at the Stevens Hotel, lasted for hours. In the room present were the chairman and the leaders of the North Carolina delegation, the late Senator John Bankhead, Governor Sparks, you, and other leaders in the Alabama delegation, Governor Cooper and leaders of the Tennessee delegation, and leaders of Mississippi, Senator Elmer Thomas, of Oklahoma, Senator Barkley, of Kentucky, and others. How helpful their cooperation was in defeating Wallace and nominating Truman for Vice President.

That night, as you remember, there were in the room representatives of some one hundred and thirty odd southern votes, who stood fast. How rapidly the hours passed. Will you ever forget about 3:30 A.M. on the morning of July 21, when all those present unanimously pledged themselves that, under no circumstances, would they cast a single vote for Wallace.

Can you ever forget on the first ballot on July 21 how close Wallace came to being nominated for vice president? Wallace 429-1/2—Truman 319-1/2—balance scattered! Then came the second ballot. Then the third ballot, when Senator Bankhead released all his delegates for Truman, and how other southern states followed, which brought about the nomination of Truman for vice-president—and how every man present kept his word and placed the interests of his country first. I was sorry I did not have a vote at that convention. But, what an honor and what *a privilege to have been there and to have been able to render even a little service.*

Yes, Frank, our people owe you and the others mentioned a lasting debt of gratitude for the great patriotic service rendered our country at the 1944 Democratic Convention. May God bless all of you and inspire the president to bring about an early and lasting peace, based on the American principles of justice, for which we fought, and upon which our country was founded.

Your friend,
Robert M. Harris

The following letters were put into the Congressional Record. The first one was written on May 15, 1947, in the United States Senate in Washington:

Dear Robert:

Let me thank you for your letter of May 12th from San Antonio, enclosing copy of your letter to our mutual friend Frank Boykin.

It is needless for me to say that I thoroughly agree with your views, and I shudder even yet to think how close we were to disaster.

Before the Georgia Delegation left for Chicago, I personally called Arnall and advised him that in my opinion and based upon the very best evidence obtainable Wallace would not be named as Vice President and urged him to consider some strong Southern man for the nomination. My efforts were in vain, as you know.

With best wishes, I am

Sincerely yours,
Walter F. George

(Lake Charles, Louisiana, May 19, 1947)

Dear Bob:

That was a fine letter you wrote Frank Boykin, and I enjoyed reading the copy.

If I never do another thing politically, I feel I have justified my political existence by being a part of the movement which prevented Wallace from being President.

With personal regards,

Sincerely,
Sam. H. Jones

My Dear Mr. Harris:

Thanks so much for your letter enclosing a copy of your letter to our mutual friend, Frank Boykin.

I certainly appreciate your kindness in sending this to me, and I have noted with much interest what you say with respect to the efforts of all of us to prevent the nomination of Mr. Wallace. I think this is one of the most valuable accomplishments of the Southern people for quite a long time.

With best wishes, I am

Faithfully yours,
Harry F. Byrd

From 1946 to 1948, Wallace was chief editor of *New Republic* magazine, a leftist socialist journal supporting the Soviet Union and critical of the Cold War. He was often quoted from a speech in 1948, in which he stated, "If I fail to cry out that I am anti-Communist, it is not because I am friendly to Communism, but because at this time of growing intolerance I refuse to join even the outer circle of that band of men who stir the steaming cauldron of hate and fear."

If it hadn't been for the Southern delegation and their wisdom, drive, and ingenuity of keeping Henry Wallace from the vice presidency for another term, he could have become our first Communist president—and our country would be drastically different today.

CHAPTER ELEVEN

Durability

On a spring day in 1945, Frank and Ocllo Boykin drove from Mobile to call on President Roosevelt, who was vacationing at Warm Springs, Georgia. He greeted them cordially and began joking about Frank's "love" slogan, as he had done often. On a more serious note, he said, "You know, Frank, I began to believe you have something there. Everything *is* made for love." He emphasized the word "is" as if he really meant it.

Though Boykins was shocked at the dead-tired appearance on the president's face, he was cheerful and talked brilliantly. Frank handed him a big twenty-five-pound frozen turkey gobbler, and FDR appeared delighted. Frank often sent turkeys and venison to the White House for him since, after many invitations to his hunting lodge, Roosevelt was always unable to make it.

After an hour or two came the goodbyes. As he was leaving, Frank called out, "Everything's made for love," not realizing that would be the last time he saw the master political showman of his time.

Several weeks later, the sad news of Roosevelt's death reached Capitol Hill. Frank told his sons, "He was a brilliant thinker and a man whose spirit showed us that work can save any situation."

Frank entered Sam Rayburn's office in the Capitol, where the talk was of a dead president in Georgia and a vice president ready to step into his shoes in Washington. It was quite dramatic: Harry Truman only met President Roosevelt twice before he died and left him with the world to run.

The legislation was in disarray and confusion. It was immersed in discussion as to which laws on the table would be passed under the new, inexperienced administration.

* * *

In February 1945, the secretary of the interior, Harold Ickes, resigned from President Truman's cabinet and unwittingly touched off a spontaneous appeal for Frank Boykin to succeed to the important post. He was a congressionally backed candidate, with 154 congressmen and eleven senators urging the new president to appoint the Alabamian to the vacancy in his cabinet. A steady stream of telegrams and letters was sent endorsing Frank for the position.

Behind closed doors on Capitol Hill, they decided to support Frank as the most logical, knowledgeable candidate for the position. Luther Patrick of Alabama pointed out that Frank's experience on the House committees—Insular Affairs, Merchant Marine and Fisheries, Public Building and Grounds, Rivers and Harbors, and Patents—had fitted him ideally for the post. Overnight, rallies of "Boykin for Secretary of the Interior" blossomed like the cherry trees around the Jefferson Memorial on the first warm days of spring.

Frank's supporters opened campaign headquarters at a leading Washington hotel, and senators and representatives from Mobile to California came to press for his appointment. Like when Frank himself was on the trail, the movement gathered momentum as it went along, catching all of Capitol Hill and the White House in its enthusiastic sweep. Meanwhile, the object of this outpouring continued to breeze through his everyday tasks with a desk littered with telegrams and letters endorsing his candidacy.

When asked what he thought about it, Frank said, "I will not accept the position if I am offered it as I am satisfied where I am so long as my people see fit to return me to Congress. I would not think of leaving Congress until I have finished the important ship sales bill of the Merchant Marine and Fisheries Committee. This alone amounts to seventeen billion dollars. And there's the harbors development program, which, to my District and State alone when completed, will amount to five million dollars."

On February 21, Frank's sixty-first birthday, the delegation that wanted him to fill the vacancy was in President Truman's office to press for his appointment. Senator John Bankhead was spokesperson for the group, which included Lister Hill of Alabama, Tom Stewart of Tennessee, John Overton of Louisiana, Olin Johnston and Burnet of Mississippi, Millard Tydings and George Radcliff of Maryland, James Eastland of Mississippi, Walter George and Richard Russell of Georgia, and Claude Pepper of Florida.

From the House came the delegation led by veteran Robert Doughton of North Carolina, chairman of the mighty Ways and Means Committee. Speaking for the group was Sam Hobbs, dean of Alabama's membership in the House. After describing Frank as having more energy than a steam engine, Hobbs continued, "He has much knowledge of the Interior Department as any man in the nation. The Department deals with nineteen separate functions. In his knowledge of forestry, conservation, water control, and wildlife, he is surpassed by no man."

President Truman listened attentively. The size of the delegation was impressive. It was the largest aggregation of lawmakers ever to visit the White House on a similar mission.

A week later, President Truman wrote Frank about why he had not given him the cabinet appointment. *"I was always of the opinion that it would be a loss to Congress to take you out of it,"* said Truman. *"Due to your seniority and familiarity with the legislative business I felt I should go elsewhere for Secretary of the Interior. The same applies to my good friend, Senator O'Mahoney of Wyoming. I believe we have a good man for the place."* On that same day, the president appointed Julius King, former chairman of the War Production Board and a TVA power expert, to the post of secretary of the interior.

* * *

During President Truman's administration, Frank vowed to get him a Missouri blue tick coon hound to sprawl about the White House grounds. Learning that the president and his wife wanted a dog around, now that they had a home with a lawn attached, Frank presented the chief executive with a breed that was named for his state. The president ended up with Old Hickory, who had the run of the White House.

One of Frank's extracurricular activities during two decades of congressional service was saving the lives of many unclaimed dogs that had been picked up on the streets of Washington and were awaiting execution in the gas chamber at the District of Columbia pound after the legal reprieve for vagrant canines. Three times a week, en route to his office on Capitol Hill, Frank would detour by way of the dog pound to look over the catch. He would select promising-looking dogs and save them by sending them to constituents without dogs. He would also give them as gifts to friends, hunters, and outdoorsmen back home. He rescued everything in the dog category, including bull dogs, Russian wolfhounds, cockers, bird dogs, hounds of every breed, whippets, Great Danes and even huskies. His humane hobby meant digging down in his own pocket and shelling out about five thousand dollars, but it paid off in dividends of happiness for the dogs, for their new owners and for the man who helped the pooches along to a better life. He made a lot of dogs and a lot of people happier. It cost Frank around seventeen dollars a piece to save a dog's life: two dollars for the pound fee and fifteen dollars express charges. But to Frank, it was a small price to pay since he believed that every dog deserved a home and a doghouse of its own.

He would stride into the big cage with the condemned unfortunates, who seemed to sense instinctively that they had found a friend for whom "Everything's Made for Love"—including dogs. This big, jovial figure and cheery "dog talk" brought a clamorous response of barks, howls, yelps and leaps. He would rub their bellies one after another, scratch their ears, and pet their backs and necks, all the while talking and "cooing" to them. Of all the dogs he rescued, declared the pound assistants, not one ever bit him or even snarled at him. They knew he was truly a dog's best friend. Unfortunately, he never knew the breed of Boykin spaniels from South Carolina that he would have fallen in love with at first sight.

They're Alabamy-bound

CONGRESSMAN Frank W. Boykin of Alabama spends more time in the doghouse than any other man on Capitol Hill. Every morning en route to his office in Washington, Boykin detours by way of the dog pound, looks over the crop of unclaimed canines awaiting execution, selects the best, and sends them to friends and constituents back home. As a result of this hobby, the lives of over 200 dogs have been saved. Boykin feels that every dog should have his own doghouse and has found that a lot of folks agree. One friend has told another, and Boykin has had requests from nearly every state, and from Chile, Africa, and Alaska. At the pound, he has found almost every breed of dog, including Russian wolfhounds, bulldogs, cockers, bird dogs, whippets, Danes, and huskies. Boykin, himself, owns more than 100 hunters, which he keeps at a lodge in Alabama, and has won many hunting trophies. His home is in Mobile and, in addition to being a lawmaker, he is a lumberman and cattle breeder. Boykin has been in Congress since 1935 and is regarded as one of the most popular men in Washington, enjoying friendships among both Republicans and Democrats.

CHAPTER TWELVE

A Dream Comes True

A new president now sat in the White House. To enlist presidential power and prestige regarding his long hoped-for construction of the Tennessee Tombigbee Canal, Frank invited a delegation of legislators and constituents to the executive mansion, where, after listening to his plea, President Truman remarked, "Frank, you do not have to sell me on that. I am as strong for the Tombigbee Canal as you are."

Late in the spring, Frank obtained the floor of the House to draw a parallel between the proposed "Ten-Tom" plan and the Erie Canal, which coupled the Hudson River with the Great Lakes, built in 1825. The famed "Wedding of the Waters," he argued, was the greatest single factor in the remarkable development and prosperity of the state and city of New York in the nineteenth century. What the Erie Canal had done for New York, the "Ten-Tom" would achieve for Alabama and her great seaport, Mobile. Its invigorating effect on the city's commerce would be incalculable by connecting Mobile with the great river systems of the Mississippi, the Ohio, the Arkansas, the Illinois and the Tennessee Rivers. It would shorten the route between Tennessee and the Gulf by six hundred miles and provide a passage for barges and vessels that rode the swift Mississippi.

On June 6, in the House of Representatives, there were many heated arguments. After beating sharp Republican opposition, the votes came for the construction of the thirty-nine-mile Tennessee-Tombigbee Canal, at a cost of $116 million dollars.

Frank never gave up and his dream finally came to be in the spring of 1946. For the previous decade, he kept the spark of this project alive when others declared it hopeless. A jubilant Frank wrote in a telegram to Mobile, "This is the greatest economic break our section of the country has ever received from Congress." Weeks later, the Senate approved a concurrent measure. Frank stood at President Truman's right hand when he attached his signature to the project for which the Alabamian had so patiently waited.

* * *

The wheel of political fortunes on Capitol Hill turns slowly, but it turns, nevertheless. The November 1946 election swept the Republicans into control of both Houses of Congress. But by January 1947, the Democrats, as the reigning victorious party, began changing heads of the all-important House committees and handing these desirable posts to their own members. Frank Boykin lost his chairmanship of the Patents Committee.

Joseph Martin of Massachusetts became the Democratic majority leader. Sam Rayburn of Texas lost his shiny new Cadillac sedan, which was one of the perks of the Speaker's high office. With it went the chauffeur to drive it and the gas and oil to run it on. (The Speaker's gavel would later be restored to Rayburn in January 1949.)

The Republicans of the Eightieth Congress assumed the reins of government and set about to win approval and popularity with the American people by the legendary route to the hearts of the nation: an income tax cut. They endorsed the largest bill, numbered HR I. The Democrats fought it feverishly. At the White House, President Truman made the threat to veto the bill, which spread through the legislative mill in record time. Frank was the only Alabama congressman to vote for the reduction. Southern newspapers wrote negatively about his vote, but he stood steadfast, saying:

> It was my vote and I tried to get a cut in the taxes for the people. I believe everybody wants taxes cut properly. I don't see how we can stand high taxes much longer.... I voted to represent. I have had more complimentary letters on it than any other vote I've ever cast in Congress. This bill will save the people of Alabama between thirty-five and fifty million dollars a year. If that's wrong, then make the most of it.

Mobile's newspaper, more foreseeing than its competitors, applauded Frank's vote and accused the other eight Alabama members who voted against the bill of "casting votes against the taxpayer" while "only Representative Boykin had the bigness to rule out cheap partisan politics for the sake of the people."

In 1948, Frank stood in the House to denounce President Truman's program of anti-lynching, anti-poll tax and anti-race segregation legislation. He was one of seventy-four Southerners who signed a pledge to oppose the Truman agenda to the finish. Being more specific, he announced, "You can bet your bottom dollar that I have organized a fight against the bill and that I will make the fight 'til my death, come hell or high water. The Truman Bill should be 'a bill to compensate rapists and murderers, their wives, their children and their families.'"

His support came via plenty of correspondences:

Selma, Ala
January 28, 1948
Hon. F. W. Boykin
House Building,
Washington, D.C.

Dear Frank:

From the old Abba days, I know that you knew your way around. Exhibit "A" shows that we are going broke day by day. Exhibit "B" shows that you are trying to help everybody, and we are proud of you, and I am glad that I cast my vote for you when you had your hat in the ring for the Senate, and am sorry that you did not make it but if you keep this up you will land it, as Big Jim says you have to run to get ready to go in. (This does not mean for one minute that I am for that so and so from the branch head) but he has something on the ball and so has the Governor from Mississippi. For the love of me I cannot see what is wrong with Harry Truman but if he vetoes another Tax reduction bill he will be headed back to Missouri. Harry is a good fellow and if you will kindly slip him a few nips of Bourbon and talk it over with him and let him know that you are in touch with the branch heads and the city slickers too and they are getting darn tired of high government spending, and the farmers are sore too about the Guano and Nitrate, and Potash that can't be bought, when at Hanover, Germany there is the largest potash mine in the world, with Alsas and Lorraine full of it too. It must be that they are too lazy to dig it and it is easier to get it from the good old U.S for free. Harry is a good fellow and means well but if he does not give us relief his chance this fall is as slim as a snowball in that well talked about place. You know Dallas County was Democratic before the Bull Mooser's (who have taken charge of the Donkey) knew anything but the GOP. In fact, we thought all Republicans were black, this is fast changing and you can hear every day someone say we hope the GOP win as they seem to have the brains and know how to run the affairs without so much turmoil.

Exhibit xyz Dog: I am ashamed to send you this one, but he sees the trend of the people and is on the band wagon while it is hot. (He was in Selma Last night full of Old Guggenheimer) and gets away with it too.

If you throw your hat in the Ring for the Senate, I will go the limit for a hitch or more.

Hoping you will find time to read this. With best personal regards,

Sincerely Yours,
Henry Jones

Congress of the United States
Office of the Democratic Whip
House of Representatives
November 3, 1948

Dear Frank:

I am very pleased to learn of your reelection to the House, and I am looking forward to our association during the next two years.

We Democrats have received a splendid tribute from the American people, and we must all work together to carry out the principles of the Democratic Party.

My congratulations to you on your splendid victory.

With kindest personal regards,

Sincerely,
John

To this letter, Frank replied:

November 8, 1948
Hon. Jon W. McCormack
House of Representatives
House Office Building
Washington, D.C.

My Dear John:

Thanks so much for your letter of November 3, which I sincerely appreciated. We had a great election, and we have a wonderful opportunity to do a lot of good. As you say, we must all work together to carry out the principles of the Democratic Party.

Congratulations to you, too, John, and I am looking forward to seeing you in January.

With warm personal regards from all of us to all of you, I am

Sincerely,
Frank W. Boykin, M.C.

The Alabama delegation at the 1948 Democratic National Convention in Chicago protested against the Truman civil rights platform. In a four-day round-up, Frank gathered 159 members of the House to sign a petition to force the Taft-Ellender-Wagner housing bill out of the Banking and Currency Committee. This measure provided the extension of financing, under loan insurance terms through the Federal Housing Administration, of five hundred thousand units of public housing from rural housing loans. It also had slum clearance features to encourage local government bodies to work with private enterprise in buying up slum areas for redevelopment.

By the end of the convention's fourth day, Frank had "sweet-talked" 205 members of the House into affixing their autographs to the petition. With the petition lacking only thirteen signatures to make it automatically operative, Speaker Martin requested a parley and agreed that the House leadership would extract the bill from committee if Frank would call off his 'war-dogs' and stop hounding House members.

* * *

The Marshall Plan was better known as the European Recovery Program; it became law in April 1948, when President Truman signed the first appropriation bill authorizing five billion dollars to help spur the industrial production of Western Europe. One of the items in the bill was a provision to give or charter 300 American-built ships to foreign nations receiving assistance under the Marshall Plan. America would load the ships with free recovery cargos but would permit European nations to man them with their foreign crews working at substandard wages and thereby throw over 20,000 American seamen out of gainful employment. Americans would then pay these nations to haul the free cargo in ships America had given them.

Reacting strongly to this a few months earlier, in July 1948, Frank led the Alabama delegation's walkout at the convention that nominated Harry Truman for the presidency, though he voted for the Missourian in November. Truman's whistlestop campaign had confounded the predictors and turned the tables on Republican candidate Thomas Dewey.

Again, Frank was not alone in believing in his actions. On November 26, 1948, he received the following letter from constituent and friend Lloyd Morgan, owner of Morgan Lumber & Manufacturing Company in Selma, Alabama:

> *Dear Frank:*
> *I was disappointed in not being able to come down to Mobile to the meeting of the State Chamber of Commerce last week.*

> *I see you are quoted in papers in the last few days as having made two statements before the Mobile Rotary Club. The first was that President Truman told you he did not believe in his Civil Rights Program any more than you did but felt that he had to embrace this doctrine for practical purposes. Your second statement was that you felt like this election was the best thing that could have happened.*
>
> *I can well believe the first statement to Chauncey Sparks four years earlier. The fact that he made such statement to you and Governor Sparks, however, brands him as a political hypocrite and I certainly cannot understand how his election could be a good thing for the country.*
>
> *In the first place I think it well to have a change occasionally anyway. Any party regardless of which it is gets rotten when it has been in power too long. The present administration has been rotten since it came into power 16 years ago. It may be, of course, that President Truman, having been brought up in the political atmosphere of the Prendergast gang, may believe double talk, double dealing and double crossing is smart politics. That is the political philosophy on which he was reared.*
>
> *I wrote you some 3 years ago that I thought President Truman would go down in history as one of the two or three weakest presidents this nation has ever had. Nothing has happened since that time to change my opinion but on the other hand plenty has happened to confirm it. I have always been an optimist, but I am wondering now whether this country will be able to survive the present trend for another four years and still retain those principles which have made it the greatest nation on earth. There seems to have been a concentrated effort for the past 16 years to scrap all the principles which made this country great and strong.*
>
> *With kindest regards to you and each of your family, I remain,*
>
> *Yours very truly,*
L.W. Morgan

The House was heating up, indeed.

CHAPTER THIRTEEN

The Movie Deal

At sixty, Frank had emerged as a national figure, and his life was exciting and enjoyable. His exuberance jetted him into the spotlight in a manner unlike anything seen in Washington in a generation. He walked with kings, queens, presidents, prime ministers, popes and head of governments, yet never lost touch with the less exalted of his friends and constituents. Worldly honors had fallen lightly on his shoulders.

He had earned all this through his own labor, and of his own hand and brain. On the way up, he had fought many a grueling battle. He had enemies, but this applied to most men struggling from the very bottom to the top and staying there.

Considering the kind of presence Frank W. Boykin was, it wasn't surprising that a deal for a movie based on his life was being worked out, in 1950, with Marshall Breedlove Productions, Inc. in Beverly Hills, California. Those involved were quite impressive names with lots of credits in their bios. Marshall R. Breedlove was producer, along with George J. O'Brien, a producer and contract actor with 20th Century Fox, who, in 1947, was in *My Wild Irish Rose*; in 1948, in the John Ford Heroin Cooper production *Fort Apache*; in 1949, in the Ford-Cooper production *She Wore a Yellow Ribbon*; and in 1950 to 1951, in his own production, *Gold Raiders*.

Franklin Adreoe was to be associate producer; he was a director at Republic Productions, Incorporated, of Studio City, California. Also included were Gordon B. Forbes, whose father was B.C. Forbes of *Forbes*

Magazine in Manhattan, New York, as the assistant head of the budget department; Harold Schuster of Los Angeles, California, a director and film editor; and Robert F. Anderson, a program manager and exploitation director of *Pantomime Quiz*, the Academy-Award winning TV program.

At that point in time, Frank was no stranger to the screen—the small screen, that is. For several years he did the Ted Mack telethon fundraiser, for which he received the following letter:

> *February 6, 1951*
> *Dear Mr. Boykin:*
> *Words fail me when I try to express my very deep appreciation for the enthusiastic support you gave me, both last year and this, toward the success of the VIP shows. You are one of the kindest, most effective, and most beloved persons it has ever been pleasured to know. Anyone who has you as an ally is fortunate indeed.*
> *Indebted to you immeasurably are the Ted Mack staff, the Women's National Press Club, and the U.S.O. Some time, I hope all of us will find a way to repay you. At least, in part.*
> *Ever so sincerely and gratefully,*
> *Hope Ridings Miller*
> *Associate Producer of The VIP Amateur Shows*

However, Hollywood was another story altogether. A response to the movie from Frank's office was typically enthusiastic:

> *May 19, 1950*
> *Mr. Marshall R. Breedlove*
> *2817 Malcolm Ave*
> *West Los Angeles 64, California*
>
> *Dear Mr. Breedlove:*
> *The Congressman received your letter as he was leaving with General Lewis A. Pick, Chief of the Army Engineers, to make a survey of the Port of Mobile, the fifth largest port in this country. He, Mrs. Boykin, Mr. Lucas (his number one Secretary,*

who has been with him for 34 years), along with little Dottie Tow, will return by car to Washington from the First District of Alabama next week. We read to him over the telephone the contract which arrived after he left, and he said it sounded okay to him. He wired you before he left, and you will hear from him immediately on his return.

He asked Jean O'Gwynn and me to assemble any data we thought would be necessary and helpful to you. This is quite a task, as there is so much here, we hardly know where to start. Mr. Walter Davenport, who wrote the story in Collier's and only stayed here a short time, told us that he found enough data in the newspaper clippings and in our scrap books to write six books, let alone one article. We will assemble all the data we can and have it ready for him to check on his return.

However, I am sending you under separate cover a composite picture of one of the greatest parties ever given in Washington. This party was given by Congressman Boykin, honoring Speaker Sam Rayburn, after they had succeeded in not bringing up a four-billion-dollar tax bill. The Congressman did not think it was possible to add a four-billion-dollar load on the taxpayers at this time, for that matter.

I am sending you several of the Congressman's speeches on Secretary Louis Johnson, the RFC; Secretary of the Treasury John Snyder; his good friend, the Honorable Stuart Symington, former Secretary of the Air Force, who has just appointed as Chairman of the National Security Resources Board to advise President Truman. Also, he made several speeches defending his friend, the Honorable John Steelman, with offices of Arkansas and Alabama, now Assistant to the President, with offices at the White House; also, a speech regarding his life-long good friend, Roy Cullen, of Houston, Texas, who has given away over 210 million dollars.

I thought maybe this would give you some idea about Congressman Boykin. I am also sending you, along with the picture of Washington's most famous party, according to Time and Life magazines, the menu of the dinner given by the

Congressman. This menu was made out of the pulp that was made from pine trees off of Mr. Boykin's land in Alabama. As you perhaps know, he has been interested in the timber, pulp and paper business, as well as the turpentine and rosin, land and livestock, for many years. He says they can do everything with a pine tree now except eat it. They make all sorts of materials from the pulp made from our pines in Alabama and the South.

Please note some of the names on this picture. Vice-President Barkley was his toastmaster. Chief Justice Carl Vinson, who served in the House with Congressman Boykin for many years, made one of the principal speeches. I am sending you a copy of the speech made by Congressman McCormack of Boston, Massachusetts, regarding this great feast. Life and Time magazines had quite a story about this famous dinner that created so much harmony. The menu fails to mention that they served a whole buffalo, along with other wild game, at this dinner where he served 903 guests in the Hall of Nations Room at the Washington Hotel, Washington, D.C.

They had Diplomats from every country on this earth, except for Russia. However, Mr. Boykin invited them, but they did not accept. Dr. Soong, Madame Chiang Kai Chek's brother, flew here for the party. You will note he had several cables from his friend, Winston Churchill. You will also note, if you examine the picture of his office in the Collier's magazine, that he has a statue of the great Churchill on his desk, along with his other treasures. There are books of letters about this party. I am going to try and find one that impressed me very much. This letter is from the Honorable Bud Dulane, head of the Pilots Union of America, with headquarters here and every Port in the Nation. Captain Bud and the Congressman have been friends since World War I, at which time Mr. Boykin was building ships at Mobile, Pensacola, and Savannah, Georgia.

I am also sending you a copy of a letter regarding the Convention, when Mr. Boykin helped stop Henry Wallace. At the time Mr. Boykin put up the fight to save the tidelands for the *states, he had hundreds of letters from practically every state in the Union and Alaska. We have copies of many telegrams, and we will prepare copies to furnish you after he checks them on his return from Alabama. For your information, the largest delegation that has ever gone to the White House, according to the record, recommending any one man for any office went in a body to see President Truman, asking him to appoint Congressman Boykin as Secretary of the Interior. This group was headed by Senator Walter George and Senator John H. Bankhead, and Congressman Bob Doughton, Chairman of the Ways and Means Committee and Dean of the Congressman, led the Members of the House to the White House to recommend the appointment of Mr. Boykin.*

I believe it will be the latter part of next week before Mr. and Mrs. Boykin, Mr. Lucas and Miss Tow return here. So, if you have any other suggestions on any data that you would like for us to get up, advise us here by Air Mail, sending copy to Mr. Boykin at 205 Government Street, Mobile, Alabama.

All of us here, including so many Congressmen from all of the states, are very pleased about your proposition to have Mr. Boykin help make a human-interest picture. We, of course know that he can do it with ease. As a matter of fact, during World War I he had a very flattering offer from Hollywood to make a picture, but he was working day and night in the manufacturing of ships, running his turpentine stills, sawmills, etc.

Since the article in Collier's by our friend, Mr. Davenport, we have received many, many letters which might be of interest to you. Also, some of his old friends have composed several songs on his slogan, "Everything's Made for Love."

Just make any suggestions that you think might be helpful and I will try to have everything in shape by the time he returns.

Sincerely yours,
(Miss) Avis Mallette

Such a gathering as described in Avis Mallette's letter was not unusual. Frank often hosted luncheons for people he never even heard of. One example was Evangelist Billy Graham, who was once a lecturer and later became a good friend of Frank's.

Frank continued throughout the years to be in contact with Winston Churchill, and one such topic they discussed centered on Billy Graham. Boykin received this letter on March 2, 1952:

Dear Sir,

The Prime Minister has asked me to reply to your letter of the 22nd of February on his behalf. He is very obliged to you for your kindness in writing him so long and interesting letter. He asked me to say that he values your kind references to himself and to his country.

Mr. Churchill's time at the present is more than usually occupied by a great pressure of important public duties and he is being obliged to forgo meeting several people, whose acquaintance, in other circumstances, it would have been a pleasure for him to make. He has asked me to say that, to his regret, he will be unable to see Dr. Billy Graham.

Yours truly,
Dwomillen Hume

On March 18, 1952, at 5:59 a.m., the Department of State received an incoming telegram from London to the Secretary of State, saying: "PLEASE PASS URGENTLY TO CONGRESSMAN FRANK BOYKIN":

Had a pleasant meeting with Dr. and Mrs. Billy Graham last Thursday. He did not raise matter of seeing Churchill, who, at any rate, would have been able to see him in view of his own previous commitments for this week.

Situation was explained to Dr. Graham and he has been most understanding. He reports meeting Eden and other members of Parliament yesterday and says he will be seeing still others today.

GIFFORD
UNCLASSIFIED

Awed by Frank's international connections, loyalty to his friends and humility in the face of success, Mr. Breedlove wrote directly to Frank, stating:

> Your story is typically American of how one individual through his own ingenuity, hard work and perseverance in spite of numerous obstacles, could develop himself as a leader of his state and country with the guiding theme 'Everything's Made for Love.' Incidentally, unless you have already attended this, I would suggest that the title 'Everything's Made for Love' be copyrighted as it might make a proper screen title. I could do it here for you should you desire.
>
> But back to the story, in the development would be included your colorful traits and characteristics which must be made vivid and alive on the screen as they have been in your real life. The early struggle, then success, with your long service to your fellow citizens and country with all the anecdotes and colorful happening will prove most instructive, humorous and entertaining. Best of all, it is an excellent portrayal of the American way of life, free enterprise, and an example of how our youth can "get out and do" and achieve success as opposed to the something for nothing attitude that is being fostered in many of our citizens today.

Using all the injection of enthusiasm of his philosophy "Everything's Made for Love," Frank made a contract with Breedlove, granting him authority to act as his exclusive agent in bringing his story to the screen, radio, television and other literary media. Also, when necessary, he would perform duties of technical director for the studio to assure accuracy and good faith in production. He would obtain the highest price and best terms possible for the story, but every offer would be submitted to Frank for approval.

Frank wrote to Breedlove personally about the project:

> *February 11, 1952*
> *Marshall R. Breedlove*

615-3/a Kelton Avenue
Los Angeles, California

My dear Mr. Breedlove:

I enjoyed my talk with you yesterday.

I had quite a group of our good friends and we were having lunch on the beautiful roof of the Washington Hotel where my wife and I live. Several of the Congressmen live there, including one of our great Members that you mentioned—our Democratic Leader, John McCormack of Boston, Massachusetts.

Until you mentioned it, I had forgotten Congressman McCormack's speech about the harmony dinner I gave honoring my beloved friend, Speaker Sam Rayburn. I had many letters about the speech that John made. He is truly a great man, and we are very close friends as he, John McCormack, has lived for many years right next to us and has even succeeded in getting my wife and me to eat these boiled New England dinners when we could be eating that great Southern cooking, but I would do most anything for this great Leader, John McCormack, and Speaker Sam Rayburn. When you and your folks come, we will meet them, also all the folks at the White House.

You referred to the great banquet we gave in the Hall of Nations room honoring Sam Rayburn. Truly, we had all the leaders of the earth and I imagine my secretary who was handling my correspondence with you at the time sent you pictures of the party. If not, I would be glad to do it now.

We had practically all the leaders of this nation and the Diplomats from all over the foreign nations except for Russia. Secretary of the Treasury, John Snyder, and John Steelman, First Assistant to the President, and a committee of about thirty, helped handle the invitations and I still think it was a mistake to have left Russia out. I find it pays to talk and maybe we could have gotten together and stopped this terrible war that is going on in Korea.

The point I was to make was this—Speaker Sam Rayburn gave a party on a two hundred foot yacht down the Potomac *about a month ago and we carried along the rescue that were made of about one or two hundred of the speeches which were made in the cocktail lounge where we had all sorts of wild game, about forty different kinds, and as our guests would come in many of them would have something to say about Sam Rayburn and would always wind up saying something about me too and in many instances they talked more about me than they did Sam. Well, I had forgotten those marvelous speeches, but we played them again down at the mouth of the Potomac where it goes into the Chesapeake Bay and where we landed and spent the night.*

I imagine John McCormack's speech states that Vice President Barkley was the Toastmaster, and Chief Justice Fred Vinson was the Principal Speaker, but we had many other speakers. Colonel Albert Ernest, who was Chairman of the entire arrangements, is my cousin from Mobile but lives in Jacksonville, Florida, where he is Vice President of the St. Regis Paper Company, the second largest paper company in the world.

I thought our Attorney General Howard McGrath made one of the best talks, but when I had the pleasure of introducing my beloved friend Sam Rayburn, Sam made a talk without any notes that will go down in history and after we heard it played many months later way out there on this beautiful yacht among the moonbeams and stars, many of the Senators and Congressman and other leaders of this nation said, "That is the speech that will be repeated when Sam goes to his Reward."

John McCormack made a dynamic speech, as well as many, many others. We have these records and when you come, we will play them and maybe some of these speeches should be in the picture.

We also had Henry Luce, Editor of Life magazine, the Chicago Tribune people. As a matter of fact, most everybody. We had Dr. T.L. Soong, Madame Chiang Kai Shek's brother, who flew here for the party from China, and Vice President Barkley figured with the people that were there and the people they represented, we had over a billion and a half or over half the people of the earth. We had my slogan, "EVERYTHING IS MADE FOR LOVE," running clear across the hall. It is claimed that it was one of the greatest groups that has ever gotten together not only in Washington but on earth.

We had a choir of about twenty-five Congressman and a little band that played all sorts of songs like, "On Moonlight Bay," "Alabama Bound," "Deep in The Heart of Texas," "Yankee Doodle Dandy," "Dixie" and many others.

It was strictly a stag affair as we just did not have room for the ladies.

I have many thoughts about this affair that might be interesting, but I have a group of men waiting for me in the outer office and I promised to get this information off to you today.

Now, I spoke to you about reading the February issue of Holiday Magazine. There is a great article in it about Mobile where you said some of the pictures would be made. The Curtis Publishing Company telephoned me to wire a few words of encouragement to our Chamber of Commerce, the day the Magazine came out. I am enclosing herewith a copy of that telegram. I am also enclosing a copy of a letter I wrote the President of the Junior Chamber of Commerce. I am also enclosing a folder of our Azalea Trail. In the middle of the picture of the three beautiful young ladies is Miss "Bebe" Betbese—Miss America 1951. She was in my office until the 6th day of May before she was selected as Miss America. In talking to Colonel Ernest over the phone this morning, he said that she told him she was going to Mobile and help run my campaign in April the same as she did in our campaign two years ago. The other two young ladies are very beautiful and they, and many, many more, would be glad to help and cooperate in making the picture a success. My entire office force is tops and are very enthusiastic over this.

A photographer from the Saturday Evening Post joined me on a hunt at the Boykin Hunting Lodge at McIntosh, Alabama, where Aaron Burr was captured, and he came all the way from

Philadelphia to take a picture of our living room at the Hunting Lodge where we have many trophies. He told me that they wanted to write a story about the place with pictures of the deer, wild turkeys, quail, doves, foxes, coons, bobcats, and bears, but I believe this picture of the living room will be in next month's issue of Saturday Evening Post.

In my judgment, the President, Mrs. Truman, Margaret, the Members of the Supreme Court, The Cabinet Members, any of the Senators or Representatives, would be glad to join us in the picture.

We have a lot of Indians, or at least part Indians, on our place on the Tombigbee River forty miles north of Mobile. Then we have many marvelous friends and, of course, a great family of Boykins and their in-laws, children and grandchildren. We raise beautiful Brahma cattle, Tennessee walking horses and we have one of the finest Arabian stallions on earth, and all in all, truly "EVERYTHING IS MADE FOR LOVE" in that unforgettable Mobile Bay country.

Now, if there is any information you want just let me know and I will get it to you by air mail.

Now, don't forget our great ship building companies, steamship companies, dry docks, aluminum company, and since I talked to you last, they are developing a hundred thirty billion tons of salt on our property between Mobile and McIntosh. We have also succeeded in getting a sixty-million-dollar rayon plant. Now the Waterman Steamship Company has a very beautiful yacht and between a hundred and fifty steamships and if we could use anything they have, it is available.

Dauphin Island is four miles out in the Gulf at the mouth of Mobile Bay. Desoto spent two years there and planted orange trees that are now as big as my body, black figs and all sorts of things. It was once the Capitol of Spain and there is a lot of history about it. Also, right across from Dauphin Island where Fort Gaines is located is Fort Morgan. These two forts are four miles apart and this is the exact spot where Farragut said, "Damn the torpedoes, full speed ahead." We own a wonderful little spot there ten miles on the Gulf and ten miles on the bay, and have an airport on our place, hard surfaced roads, and a hotel with over a hundred rooms, and fifteen or twenty cottages, and the prettiest beeches in the world. All of these things might be helpful to you.

North of Fort Morgan on the eastern shores of Mobile Bay, just across from the great city of Mobile, is the famous Spanish fort where the last battle between the States was fought. There are thirty-five miles of breastwork there, tons of bullets, arrow points, the famous Jackson Oak where the Peace Treaty was signed between us and the Indians. A few miles further up is the famous Boatyard Lake where we had the biggest Indian massacre ever recorded. I believe our history books will show that between eight hundred and a thousand soldiers, men, women and children were scalped and killed.

Then a little further up at McIntosh, Alabama, is a beautiful old log Methodist Church. The logs are had hewed. Captain Gaines and his party waited all night in the old church and remember that was in 1806 and that is where they captured Aaron Burr after he had killed Alexander Hamilton.

Since I talked to you several months ago about this picture, the Humble Oil Company, the Hunt, the Carter, and the Gulf have brought fifty or sixty wells down in the First District of Alabama, the District I have the honor to represent. The Humble Oil Company has just brought in a gusher at Brewton, Alabama. I am telling you this as we might be able to use this great machinery in the picture. The Humble is putting down a sixteen thousand foot well a few miles East of McIntosh, Alabama, in a vast swamp, big trees, and many lakes, and it is between the Alabama and Tombigbee Rivers. There is what is called a cut-off between these two rivers that they claim was dug by the Indians. That, too, could be used, this and so many other things.

By the way, I will also include in the information I am sending you a new map of the State of Alabama as it not only has some very beautiful pictures on it but this map will give you an idea about the Gulf, the Bay, and Rivers and other streams. We could take pictures of people fishing at Dauphin Island, Fort Morgan, or in our own lakes at McIntosh. We could take pictures of people catching shrimp by the ton with nets, dipping up crabs and the finest oysters in the world.

I, of course, did not know just what you all have in mind, but I thought I would tell you some of these things that might be helpful.

Also, we have the finest fox hounds in the country. My brother, R.N. Boykin, caught over 160 foxes last year. We also have beautiful bird dogs and some of the finest coon and cat dogs in the country. You, of course, understand you use walkers to hunt foxes, red bone and blue tick and black and tan hounds for coons. We had a hunt one day after Christmas at our Hunting Lodge at McIntosh and killed nine deer and 17 wild turkeys. That night we went coon hunting down on the lakes and rivers near the corn plantation and caught thirty-two coons. It took a pickup truck to haul them and some of the coons weighed seventeen pounds, so you can see it is a hunter's paradise. I think one of the most fascinating things in the world is a coon hunt. I believe we could have a marvelous scene with the dogs running the coons, treeing them and bagging them with lights to show the dogs, the hunters and the coons. Then when we make the coons jump out of the tree, they fight and a coon in a dynamite.

Now, don't forget Sam Rayburn particularly would be glad to help, and what I started to say while I was dictating this letter to you, Mr. Albert Day, Director of the Fish and Wildlife Service, Department of the Interior, came in. I am chairman of the Subcommittee of the Merchant Marine and Fisheries Committee that handle wildlife. We have at another place we own all sorts of wild ducks, pheasants, turkeys and quails. As a matter of fact, we turned over 200 coveys this fall. This spot is at Calvert, Alabama, between McIntosh and Mobile. Mr. Day and his great organization might help out on this picture *as everybody is interested in the great work he is doing, and he has the whole United States, as you know.*

Anyway, the judgment, everybody in Washington and Alabama, or almost anywhere else, will cooperate with us and Colonel Albert Ernest will run the whole show if you don't watch out. I am looking at a picture of him now with a Texas hat on, rifle in his hand, and his foot on a big black bear that he killed at McIntosh, Alabama, on the Tombigbee River a few years ago.

I was in a show to raise money for the Heart Fund, along with about forty other Congressmen. We had a show in Constitution Hall here and had an overflow group, including the President and our leaders. Then we went to New York and Speaker Rayburn could not go so I acted as Speaker for him to make the other Congressman behave. Some young lady that was in the theatre, whom I never met, composed a song about me. They call it "EVERYTHING IS MADE FOR LOVE," and I am enclosing a copy of it and return it to me as soon as you finish it. Some man with a good voice in New York made a record of it and we played it Christmas Day in Mobile, and we thought it was pretty good.

We have at Mobile facing on Mobile Bay the great Brookley Air Depot, the largest installation of its kind in this country. They have every kind of airplane that is made, hundreds of hundreds of them from the smallest to the largest. They work about fifteen thousand people there. We can use any planes or any part of this great Air Depot that you can make fit into the picture.

We have at Mount Vernon, Alabama, twenty-five miles North of Mobile an old Barracks, forty miles of which is enclosed by brick walls. It is a beautiful place, and it is the spot where the great Indian Chief Geronimo was held in captivity for many, many years. He and hundreds of his tribe moved from Mount Vernon to Oklahoma. All that part of Alabama was in the Louisiana Purchase.

> *I also forgot to mention that Fort Morgan where we have the hotel is the place where our great, great grandmothers landed, and if you know that part of the history of the country, they were called the Casket Girls. I believe it would be a great thing to reproduce that part of Fort Morgan. I would be glad to send you the data on this.*
>
> *With every good wish, I am*
>
> *Sincerely your friend, Frank W. Boykin*

On May 21, 1953, Mr. Breedlove wrote to Frank telling him:

> *...negotiations are underway with a major studio for a deal whereby we can lease space and facilities and arrange for distribution of the film under their organizational setup. The studio executive has demonstrated considerable interest in the project. He saw the publicity regarding it last week and is now investigating the possibility of working out a mutually acceptable plan of production with my company. Under this plan his studio would lease space and equipment to us, would generally supervise the production, and would follow through with the release of the picture to theatres in this country and abroad.*
>
> *They are also interested in participating financially, with a percentage of stock coming to them in proportion to the amount of money advanced. I've told them that we were planning on $900,000.00, which, as I explained to you, contained a contingency amount which would assure an outstanding finished product. Should we work out a satisfactory plan this total amount probably could be scaled down to about $750,000.00 to $800,000.00. Upon receipt of finished script 5% of the actual outlay is due. That would mean that you, Frank, and your associates would have to come in at about 7 or 8 dollars to $1.00 subscribed by the studio.*
>
> *We are in an excellent bargaining position now. The transition to wide-screen and 3-D plus inroads of television has left a shortage of product and a picture of this nature*

would be received with open arms. Also, I note Mr. Eisenhower has been interested in getting the industry to do exactly what we are doing. Produce pictures that will help build relations between Western countries, besides being good entertainment for consumption at home and abroad. We are in an enviable spot now if we can only follow through "fastest with the moistest," or better still, the best damn picture that has come out of Hollywood in many years.

The one and only phase now is that of financing, and with the possibility of assistance from the studio predicated upon our people coming through at the same time, then, truly, "Everything's Made for Love," will take on even a bigger and better meaning, plus the reality of it reaching the millions of people who will view it.

The screen story was written by Marshall R. Breedlove, from 1950 to 1953, and titled *Everything's Made for Love!*, based on the life of the Honorable Frank W. Boykin, a member of Congress. It was dedicated, "To the members of the Congress of the United States of America and to all men who have dedicated their lives to the service of their fellowman, their country, and their God—appreciation is gratefully acknowledged for their unselfish devotion to duty and for their whole-hearted cooperation which made this picture possible."

As the news spread to newspapers around the country, the *Atlanta Journal* had the following headline: *"EVERYTHING'S MADE FOR LOVE."*

Rep. Boykin of Bama to Star in Own Film

WASHINGTON (AP) Rep. Frank Boykin of Alabama said today he has yielded to Hollywood pressure to film the story of his life. Now 68 and silver haired, the one-time water boy on a railroad said the script is written and the contract awaits signature. He declined the name of company.

He said filming will begin when this session of Congress ends and will include a scene re-enacting his proposal to his wife, after jumping, from a horse to the train she was riding through Malcolm, Ala.

"Everything is for Love" has been his motto for forty years, he said. It has been booming in capital corridors since he came to the House from Mobile, Ala, 18 years ago.

BOYKIN SAID the filming would be done in his Alabama Congressional District (the First and in Washington).

The movie would depict Boykin from the time he got his first job as a water boy on a railroad through his business career in real estate, farming and timber and his 18 years in the House of Representatives.

"Everything's Made for Love" is Boykin's trademark.

He uses it as a greeting and his office staff can tell when he is approaching. From far down the wide corridors of the House Office Building his deep voice can be heard greeting friends with "Howdy Partner" and then "Everything's Made for Love!"

Boykin said he will make appearance in the picture, but that a professional actor will be chosen to play the regular role.

ONE SCENE, Boykin said, will show him shooting wild turkeys from a moving automobile on his game reservation at McIntosh, Alabama. Another will show Boykin jumping from a horse to a moving train. Boykin said he did just that in proposing to his wife.

She was going through Malcomb, Ala., on a train that wasn't going to stop. Boykin said he wanted to propose so he rode his horse beside the train and hopped aboard.

With all the articles written, Frank received letters from wannabe actors and songwriters, many of whom sent bios and lyrics to a theme song titled "Everything's Made for Love." Perhaps one of the best was the following:

May 21, 1953
Honorable Frank W. Boykin,
Congressman from Ala.
Washington D.C.

Dear Frank:

The enclosed clipping noting your new venture into movie-life was very interesting to me. I know of no one whose life should be filmed with so much interest, experience and courage as your life is made up of.

I am very happy that we are noted among some of your oldest friends. I am sure those in my family who are gone would also have been thrilled to have read this account about you.

I trust that those taking care of the filming of your life history will not overlook many things for which you are due a lot of credit, particularly that you came up "the hard way." I know that you will get a laugh out of this: don't forget to remind them of our birthplace, "Fairford."

I have overlooked advising you that the favor I asked of you some time has materialized and not only am I grateful to you, but also my niece's husband.

Wishing you continued success and especially good health, I remain,

Sincerely your friend,
Ruby Delokery

The following was written in response:

May 25, 1953
Mrs. Ruby Highnote Delokery
C/o Mobile Steel Company, Inc.
Mobile, Ala.

Dear "Miss. Ruby":

Frank is attending the atomic gun experiment in Nevada and is expected back tomorrow. In his absence, I am acknowledging receipt of your good letter of May 21st, with enclosed clipping from the Mobile Press. I am so glad you sent us this clipping with Frank's picture, as the earlier edition of the Press which we received did not have the picture. I think the picture and the caption are downright clever. You may remember that right above Frank in the picture is a framed picture showing Howard Chandler

Christie, the famous artist, talking to Marvin McIntyre, who was President Roosevelt's Secretary. Christie was telling McIntyre of Frank's first visit to New York when he had to get him a date. The date happened to be Theta Bara, the famous vamp of her day, and all of us were getting a terrific kick out of the story, including Frank, and just about that time the photographer snapped the picture. Frank's life story will be one which will have played down and not colored up, as most of them must be. I am sure no story of Frank's life would be complete without a lot of it being devoted to his early life in Fairford. It might interest you to know that we received a very interesting letter from Devereux Lake, a graduate of Vanderbilt University, who lived in Fairford in 1896 and 1897, and reminded Frank of good many incidents that occurred when Frank was about twelve or thirteen years old.

We are so happy to learn that your niece's husband's matter was taken care of. We are holding your letter for Frank's personal attention, and I know he will deeply appreciate it.

With kind personal regards, I am

Sincerely yours
Alphonse Lucas, Secretary

The following two letters arrived from Breedlove as the film project seemed to progress:

P.O. Box 4137
West Los Angeles 24
California
October 29, 1953

The Honorable Frank W. Boykin
Admiral Semmes Hotel
Mobile, Alabama

Dear Frank:
I appreciate very much your last two letters and the words of encouragement that you sent. Believe me, I needed them

after receipt of the letter from our friend Albert Ernest. I've tried to arrive at the cause of his reaction, but I am at a loss for an answer.

Needless to say, my entire organization was somewhat shocked as it was far from what was anticipated. I can only attribute it to his not being orientated on this project plus a misunderstanding of the methods and techniques of motion picture production and financing. Maybe it would have helped if I had met and discussed it with him on my trip East last Spring.

However, Frank, I sincerely hope that this approach has not caused any undue embarrassment to you—as that would defeat the purpose of the entire picture. It is gratifying to know that George Bagnall, former Vice President of United Artists and an outstanding leader in the motion picture industry for over thirty years, stated that in his opinion my plans and organization were as sound as any he had ever seen in all his years in this industry and that he would state in writing over his letterhead should I need it. Also, Frank, the legal and financial assistant to John Ford and Meriam Cooper has agreed to come with me when his services are needed. He is an exceptionally good authority on motion picture financing, and he has spent considerable time advising me. He also maintains that when we get the shooting script the remainder of the financing will not be too formidable an undertaking. As mentioned before, this script requires the services of a professional screen writer under contract. I've revised my estimated cost down and believe that I could get an adequate script for about $8000.00 to $9000.00.

That's what I'm working on now. I am pushing this with all our combined efforts. I'll do everything possible to push it through before you return to Washington. It looks more encouraging out here and I'm meeting next week with a top producer who may want to co-produce it with me.

Contrary to popular belief, most of the money for motion picture financing comes from the East—from the Chemical Bank of New York and Boston, the Hellar Company of

Chicago and our own Bank of America on the West Coast, plus individuals who are willing to invest. However, the Banks usually enter the picture only after the shooting script has been obtained.

I am enclosing a clipping regarding the filming of the life of Marshall Tito of Yugoslavia here in Hollywood. Please note that the financing is by the Yugoslav government. That's awful tough competition for a guy who's trying to bring the public's terrific success story under the American way of life. But, Frank, if it's the will of God, I'm going to do it, but I also need a little help. I couldn't ask for any better co-operation that that which you have given me. When I first started on my quest for a real-life story as a vehicle for my picture, I never dreamed I'd be so fortunate. It far exceeds my greatest expectations and I know that with your continued assistance my organization will bring to the screen one of the outstanding pictures of our time.

Frank, from the beginning I've maintained that you should personally not put up any of the required money for several reasons. However, due to the unique nature of the story, it would not be contrary to good taste and not be the exception to the usual approach if local successful citizens or in some instances, the Chamber of Commerce

advanced a portion of the financing. In fact, it would add a great deal to the over-all project should this happen. However, I don't want to make any move that might hurt us.

I will continue the fight on this end. Have made a few changes in my organization for the better. Jack Moffitt is currently doing a script for MGM but is ready to start at short notice. I'm enclosing a clipping from the Hollywood Reporter regarding Harold Schuster's success on his last picture. He's finishing another tomorrow and is anxiously awaiting the signal to start ours. George O'Brien joins them in sending their warmest regards.

Frank, this is one of the finest teams ever to collaborate on such a picture. In addition to their being sound and solid citizens, previous pictures they have made have won Academy

Awards and some have grossed upward $8,000,000.00. Besides they will have their hearts in the making of this picture. Hollywood's greatest have come from such a beginning that this will be another one. We'll have the American Legion, our Churches and schools behind us on this. Too, we want every individual who sees it to feel that this way of life provides an equal opportunity in our country for him to personally to enjoy, if he's willing to work and sacrifice to obtain same. It should be an inspiration to all who see it. There is no doubt to its eventful conclusion. A former college classmate of mine forwarded a four-column article from Winston-Salem, N.C. Journal and Sentinel of August 23, 1953, entitled "Tar Heel Acquires Film Rights to Life of Fabulous Congressman." It was an excellent article with the best picture of you that I've seen. I believe their Washington Correspondent, Miss Eleanor Nance, wrote it. I'm using it in my brochure when talking to the studios and other interested parties.

Frank, if you and your family continue to collect background information, it will assist greatly when the writer and I come. We will exert every effort to make it before the end of November. In the meantime, I'd love to hear from you and any further developments. I'll keep you informed from here.

My warmest regards to Mrs. Boykin and all your family. Also, to Mr. Lucas. Looking forward to seeing you soon.

Cordially yours,
Marshall R. Breedlove

P.O. Box 4137
West Los Angeles 24
California
February 2, 1954

The Honorable Frank W. Boykin
Representative in Congress
Room 412, Old House Office Building
Washington, D.C.

Dear Frank:

It was a real pleasure seeing you in Washington after the Holidays and talking to you by phone last week. Lunching with you, Congressman Rivers and Mr. Douglas Walford was a special treat. Sorry I had a mild touch of the flu and hope I didn't pass it on to anyone.

Frank, I would surely enjoy being there to meet with you and Speaker Joe Martin, The Honorable Alben Barkley, Billy Graham and all the other fine people you mentioned. I know that this is probably the most important session being done by yourself and the others in transgressing party lines to bring to the American people a legislative program that will continue to protect our status as a leader among the free nations. As you know, this can only be done by a strong and unwavering belief in our American heritage, the dignity of the individual, and his rights to work, live, and worship God as he chooses. Regardless of any business affiliations we may have, I want you to know how appreciative my associates and I are of your efforts on behalf of those principles on which this country was founded. Our good wishes, prayers, and highest hopes are with you currently.

Now to give you a resume of progress made on the film "Everything's Made For Love." First, every studio in Hollywood has been contacted with reactions ranging from "not interested in this type of picture as it does not fit into our program" to "Yes, we're interested—bring us the shooting script and we'll negotiate at that time for use of studio facilities, personnel, production assistance, financing and a distribution release." None would advance the cost of obtaining the shooting script.

Hence, we're way ahead, in that a good deal of groundwork has been laid prior to that stage. Now this is confidential as the studios are averse to any publicity until the actual contract has been signed. Too, it might serve to disrupt negotiations at one studio if they hear that you're contacting others. These are the reactions:

Republic Studios: Highly interested. They are willing to provide studio facilities, production assistance and a release. Provided we come up with a good script. They like my personnel and my approach. Will not help defray expense of obtaining shooting script, but willing to advise until that phase is completed.

Warner Brothers Studios: Not for us currently. However, door is open. Come back when script is completed. Check with us if you complete film before signing with someone else.

Allied Artists: Prospects good after shooting script phase. My Director, Harold Schuster's, last picture "Jack Slade" was their top money maker over last six-year period (see clipping enclosed). Also, the agency which handled that independent package is handling mine.

Paramount Studios: Prospect is very encouraging especially if I come up with a script suitable for their contract stars. I'm contemplating possibility of starring Charlton Heston, one of their players. If he likes the shooting script, then this would be a strong possibility. My director recently directed him another picture. So, this is extremely good.

RKO Studios: Negative currently. Open for further negotiation.

Twentieth Century Fox Studios: Negative. Open for further negotiation.

MGM Studios: Negative. Open for further negotiation.

So, frank, this is the picture. Contact was made with top executives in every case.

The best possibility for the film is with Republic Studios, who is highly interested in the project. Franklin Adreon, one of the producer-directors, thought it to be a sound project and would like to work out a co-production/distribution deal. The shooting script would have to be developed prior to a firm commitment. Mr. Jack Baker, vice president in charge of studio operations, and Mr. Adreon volunteered their services in the development of the script to insure an adequate property from their standpoint.

The surveying of all possible sources of financing for the script is being done and should break the bottleneck.

In March and April, the resultant local and national publicity will coincide with your campaign—which should be in May. At that time, they could be shooting the picture, which will not hurt your reelection.

With an early fall release, I plan to take advantage of the extreme interest being created in the national elections to ensure a good box office turn out for our picture. Too, I'm planning a tie-in with our schools whereby all school children can, by seeing the picture "Everything's Made for Love," get an authentic portrayal of how a citizen gets to Congress and the work he does while there as a representative of his district. This should serve to focus attention on the duly elected representatives as the true servants of the people under our constitutional government.

Dramatizing the story will give the theater-going public an entertaining film of complete Americans and a story which proves that by living your motto one can have a happy family, business, and political life.

My organization stands ready to move on the following schedule contingent on the success you have this week:

- *(1) February – April: Preproduction phase. Do additional research, write shooting script.*
- *(2) May: Shooting phase. Shoot film in Mobile and Washington D.C.*
- *(3) June – August: finish film. Edit, adapt music, sound recording, make prints, preview for audience reaction, make final changes and corrections. Prepare for early fall release.*

Harold Schuster, who did such a good job on his picture "Jack Slade" for Allied Artists, wants to make this his next picture. The Wall Street Journal reported that when news of earnings of that picture was released it caused Allied Artists stock to jump three points. So, he's very much in demand now!

Jack Moffitt has been alerted and is keeping the period open for writing the script. Attached are also news clippings on his latest writing exploits along with copies of his column "The Cracker Barrel" from the Los Angeles Herald Express. So many top people have commended me on getting such a top caliber writer as Jack for the script.

The Mitchell Gertz Agency, which is handling Harold Schuster, has offered their services in packaging the deal and negotiating for best possible release. I have been assured that once the shooting script phase has been accomplished, that with my qualified organization, studio and/or bank financing can readily be arranged for the balance.

When I get your call this week, I will immediately forward the necessary information and papers for executing the transaction.

My best regards go with you, Mrs. Boykin, and your family on your return to Alabama.

May your efforts be rewarded by the most successful campaign ever. That you will return to Washington I have no doubt, but even more important is the wonderful message we can bring to the world through your example in living the Golden Rule or more aptly stated by yourself "Everything's Made for Love." Good Luck and may God Bless You. I'll be awaiting your call.

Yours sincerely,
Marshall R. Breedlove

The last letters of any consequence, on record, regarding the movie were the above one dated February 2, 1954, from Marshall R. Breedlove and the one below, from February 3, 1954, from Frank W. Boykin:

February 3, 1954
Mr. Ben McPherson
c/o Mrs. Hazel Gentry
1206 Wexham Way
Inglewood, California

Dear Mr. McPherson:

I have your letter of January 24th. Sorry to learn that you have been confined to the hospital but glad you have now been discharged and are slowly getting your strength back.

We have been too completely swamped with Congressional work to give any time to the movie; however, Colonel Breedlove called me from Los Angeles several days ago, and he's still interested in making the movie. I have received scores of songs which I am holding in a file until such time as there may develop the possibility of using them.

With every good wish, I am

Sincerely yours,
Frank W. Boykin, M.C.

Marshall R. Breedlove also wrote in a letter dated February 24, 1954, that they were investigating the possibility of casting Will Rogers, Jr. or Charlton Heston to play Frank Boykin and of having Frank appear in the picture.

There was no other correspondence found regarding the movie or if it was ever made.

CHAPTER FOURTEEN

Labor

In 1950, during the Korean War, a newspaperman asked Frank a challenging question: "Congressman, just what do you construe the duties of a congressman to be?" Boykin replied:

> Pull as many wires as you can to get private industry to move into the district of the congressman. I personally think I've done a top job there. That means jobs for skilled and unskilled labor. It means that the unions have an opportunity to organize those who work in those industries; it means that more prosperity comes into the area. I think that any conscientious congressman should vote for all measures that aid the material well-being of his constituents. I think that federal housing is needed here and I have made enemies with the real estate groups because I urge such housing and have voted for it. I am dead opposed to socialistic schemes, but I do think the federal government should have yard sticks to determine what a fair price for the monopoly industry to charge the consumer.
>
> I'd done a good job of getting big industry to build and get established in our district, that's true up to a point but as Al Jolson used to say, "YOU AIN'T SEEN NOTHING YET." Sure, I entertain lavishly, because I believe that it takes more than a cold-blooded business approach to get people to like you and the people you

represent. So far, this approach of mine has paid dividends to everyone who lives in my district. I'm going to keep on being friendly with people from all walks of life. My office is always working on war casualty cases; we foot the bill for finding the loved ones of those who have been wounded or lost in Korea. We never ask, "Can you afford the cables?" We do the job. That's my idea of a congressman doing his job and you tell your readers; I love doing it no matter the cost. I wouldn't change a thing I've done; maybe I've been too eager to help some who did not deserve, but hell! If I screened all of them and had case histories made there would be no fun in living and helping other people to live. As for Fulton Lewis, Jr., Drew Pearson and other journalists, they're paid to sensationalize the news and God love them, maybe I'm helping them draw better pay.

An article that ran at nearly the same time stated:

Labor's Salute to a Friend

Congressman Frank W. Boykin has given Mobile Labor another "Big shot in the Arm." Following the acquisition of the many millions of dollars to Mathieson Chemical Plant in McIntosh, which made necessary the Alabama Power Company's tremendous new plant in Salco, Frank has persuaded our English friends to build their rayon plant in Mobile County. It is presently negotiating with other prospective large industries for their locating at or near Mobile.

We all know that it was by Congressman Boykin's personal efforts that Brookley Field is in Mobile, employing between fifteen and sixteen thousand civilian workers with annual pay roll of over fifty million dollars.

> Had it not been for Frank Boykin, it is our opinion that the Mobile Paper Company would not be operating today.
>
> And what does this mean to Labor? It means jobs and good permanent jobs. Can any fair-minded laboring man say that Frank Boykin is not a true and loyal friend to labor?

We take off our hats to Frank for the grand job he has done for the people of his Country, his District, and his State. We have a great deal of gratitude to Frank, particularly for what he has done for Labor—LONG MAY HE LIVE AND PROSPER!

Congressman Boykin was infinitely proud of his work toward the industrial expansion in the Mobile region and northerly along the Tombigbee. With uncanny correctness, he had envisioned things to come, and an empire of industry was now taking shape rapidly. Frank laid cornerstones, as well as dedicating dams, bridges, post offices, high schools and almost everything that called for dedicating. It was as if he never stopped and couldn't be stopped, like a force of nature.

In 1951, with sixteen years of continuous service in the House behind him, Frank became the dean of the Alabama delegation in the House of Representatives. His seniority on this plateau was something to be marveled at. He was already inducted into the inner circle. A member of the House, who was from Missouri and had twenty-four years seniority, later observed, "I've served in the House for a very long time and I have known many people in Washington and on Capitol Hill, but my friend Frank Boykin, in less than six months from the day he entered Congress, knew more people, and is now known by more than I am after a quarter of a century in the House."

The year Grace Boykin was born was also the year for Frank's 1952 reelection campaign, which was a sizzler. In past campaigns, he had remained in Washington, but two opponents were squawking at him throughout the district so he came home and campaigned vigorously. He was on top of his game.

At the time, the following statement was written and delivered by the Honorable Frank W. Boykin:

After the Civil War ended a great portion of the South was impoverished, many of our homes and farms were in ruins, our economy had been shattered, and as a result all of our citizens of both races suffered. The courage and fortitude of our people in our rebuilding is now a matter of history. Seldom has such a gigantic task of rehabilitation been attempted without outside help. The people of the South had no Marshall Plan—no E.C.A. Only in the past 30 or 40 years have we completely emerged from the havoc and destruction wrought by Civil War.

The progress which has been made in all phases of our economic life has been astounding.

I doubt that there is another area of the United States where there is more real harmony and understanding between the people of both the white and colored races. During my entire lifetime this harmony has existed and as a result our people have advanced and prospered and improved their educational, cultural, and economic conditions.

I believe now, as I have always believed, that the solution of our problems lies in the continued goodwill and harmony between the leaders of both races, which has existed down through the years. With the advent of the new industrial era in South Alabama, there will be greater prosperity and job opportunities for all—for our children and our children's children. Let us continue to work together people of both races—and help give Alabama her rightful "place in the sun."

Frank's message of peace and harmony would also spread to the international community, as the letters below show:

Daniel A. Poling
Chairman & Editor
Christian Herald Magazine
November 30, 1953

Dear Friend:

As you know, I am concerned that peace shall reign in the Middle East. I am no less intent on our great nation sparing no efforts to foster friendship between Israel and the Arab states and to make available all necessary resources, both material and spiritual, to both Arab and Jew in rebuilding this blighted area of the world. Like you, I want the Holy Land to be a source of blessing, not warfare, for the entire Mediterranean Basin.

The importance and urgency of a just solution to the Palestine conflict at this very hour impel me to share with you this excellent book, **The Palestine Problem Today: Israel and Its Neighbors**, *written by my good friend and esteemed colleague in the Christian Ministry, Dr. Carl Hermann Voss. When you read this book, you will find that Dr. Voss has, in precise and scholarly fashion, given clear, cogent answers to some of the most vexing questions in the Palestine situation. Excellent maps and well-chosen illustrations aid him in these eighty well-written pages to encompass a wide variety of issues, ranging from the Arab refugees to Soviet intentions in the Near and Middle East, from so called "dual loyalties" to Israel's potential as a citadel of democratic hope and faith in that feudal area. You will find this book a mine of objective information and of inestimable value in preparing articles and addresses.*

Accept this book with my compliments and know that I shall be interested in your reactions to its compelling message.

You know that, as always, I send you my warm personal regards.

Sincerely,
Daniel A. Poling

December 7, 1953
Mr. Daniel A. Poling,
Chairman and Editor,
Christian Herald,
27 East 39th St.,
New York 16, N.Y.

Dear Mr. Poling:

The book titled "THE PALESTINE PROBLEM TODAY" which you so kindly sent has just been received.

I have not had the time to read it, but I know that I shall find it both interesting and informative and I do appreciate your thoughtfulness in sending it to me.

With all good wishes, I am

Sincerely yours,
Frank W. Boykin

Before the election was held, the old commentator Drew Pearson rushed to kick the lion before he was dead. Utilizing his syndicated column and network program, he made Frank's re-election a national issue, stooping to a new low by intimating that his whipping boy might die before he could be sworn in for a new term if, by some remote chance, he won.

After hearing the commentary, a family member wrote a blistering response that was sent immediately to Mr. Pearson:

May 12, 1952
Dear Mr. Pearson:

I was not unfortunate enough to have heard your broadcast of last evening. I have just been informed of your prediction that FRANK BOYKIN will not serve this term out.

Mr. Pearson, I don't know who has given you the authority to act as God or the right to trample the hearts of so many thousands of people who know and love FRANK BOYKIN for the very great man he is. If men but grew in statue simultaneously with the bigness of their hearts and with the kindness they bestow, you would be but a toad frog and FRANK BOYKIN as the great giant redwood of the forest.

I am a BOYKIN and that is said with great pride. Pride a word evidently not in your vocabulary, since you take no pride in the harmony of friends and close family relationship, so necessary to the American way of life...of which you are no advocate. To love thy neighbor as thy self.

My husband, FRANK BOYKIN'S son, has done more for this land in one day than you in twenty-five years. We live in a five-room prefabricated house and his salary is eighty-five dollars per week, and not the thousands you have stated we BOYKINS possess on your foul-mouthed radio program. The richness that FRANK BOYKIN has brought my house has been with his love and friendliness. I'll bet your children don't think that of you.

My mother-in-law is the finest lady in the world, and you have hurt her heart many times with your false accusations... and all our hearts...for which I'm sure the God you are so hard trying to portray would like you to get down on your hands and knees and beg forgiveness.

You have been misinformed. God is kind and just and fortunately, though, this great land of ours is guided by that powerful unseen hand from above which has kept us a democracy for so long...and not by Drew Pearson's Predictions of things to come.

But you see, Mr. Pearson, you have been wrong before, many times...especially pertaining to FRANK BOYKIN...for example, the election just past. Your superficial pride was just deflated, and you had to come back with the meanest thought that only you could possess.

I am a lady innately and conductively but if I were a Navy man, I could really tell you what most people in the nation think of you.

There has always been someone (Ex. Hitler) in countries who try to set themselves above the average human being and when a good man gets ahead—this jealous, malicious person is the first always to attack orally. But I see, MR. PEARSON, you always keep your distance.

NOW, FRANK BOYKIN AS A MAN.

He doesn't have to lend from or buy friends. Everybody who has ever been within range of his voice is a willing friend unless they are your type whom the prince and power of this earth rules.

> *He is—without competition—the brightest ray of sunshine ever to beam forth from Alabama or any other state. He is the kind of man whom people come from miles to see because he radiates a goodness and friendliness for his fellow man surpassed by no one. He has more friends in this one county in Alabama than you have in this whole nation. He should be in the White House and not Congress.*
>
> *I hope, Mr. Pearson, since you have had so much time to blast the Boykin family, that you will have time for a letter from a Boykin. Because one of these days when you are a mean, broken, crabby, friendless old man you will remember that this BOYKIN predicted that.*
>
> *As a Father, FRANK BOYKIN is the kind of man who sits up all night when there is sickness or a death and prays...a feat of which I doubt you are capable.*
>
> *As a friend, he is friend to everyone...man or beast. The man in overalls, the man in tuxedo, the lady in furs, the lady in rags. Everybody loves him. For him...EVERYTHING IS TRULY MADE FOR LOVE.*
>
> *If your prediction, which only death can fulfill comes true—and which we pray every night and day will not come to pass, he will go to take his place among the stars in the Heavens, for he is a bright and shining star...and you, Mr. Pearson, will go the other way with everybody's blessing.*
>
> Very truly yours,
Mrs. R. Boykin

But the voters were not beguiled by Pearson's remarks. Newspaper post-mortems estimated that Pearson's attacks had led to over 3,000 votes for the winner. The two hopefuls, who had synchronized their attacks on the theme "Boykin must go!," were overwhelmed by Frank's 9,000 votes more than his rivals. Frank proved he was still the top vote-catcher in Alabama's First District.

Pearson was consistent and seemed to be Frank's personal paparazzi from the day he took his seat in the House. Senator Thomas Henning's of Missouri was a close friend of both Frank and Drew Pearson. One day he asked Drew, "Why do you continue to persecute Frank Boykin?" According to Henning's, the reply was, "Why, Tom, Frank Boykin is such a good copy. If I wrote two columns of something good about him, the people wouldn't read or believe it." Reputedly, on another occasion, Pearson observed, "I have done everything I could to destroy him, and I have come to the conclusion that Frank Boykin is indestructible."

For the 1952 elections, the Republicans had picked their standard-bearer: General Dwight D. Eisenhower, who stepped onto the scene with all the glamour of his crusade in Europe that crushed the Nazis. Eisenhower was a shoo-in the moment the Republicans tapped him. They couldn't miss. It was an old, unbeatable political gimmick: nominating a triumphant general to head the party's bid for the White House. Historically, generals were irresistible vote-getters. Eight times, generals had led political parties to victory. There was something about a soldier...and that was why, repeatedly, the American people had given their hearts and votes to soldier-candidates.

With Eisenhower out front for the Republicans, the Democrats might well have shut up shop, gone home and saved their convention and campaign expenses, but after five days of ballyhoo, they saddled their slate with Adlai Stevenson of Illinois and Senator John Sparkman of Alabama, neither of which had the spark to capture the office. Frank supported the Stevenson-Sparkman campaign team by giving several speeches for them in Southern Alabama. Alabama not only escaped the Eisenhower deluge but, by a 2-1 majority, voted for the Democratic ticket. Still, the Republicans had not only swept Eisenhower into the presidency but seized majority control of the House of Representatives.

Cheers over the election were still going on when Frank went on the air to urge his constituents to unite behind General Eisenhower. "Let us all join in prayer for a successful administration for the common good," he said. In the same vain he wrote the president-elect, who replied, "Thank you for your pledge of cooperation. It is encouraging to know that in the difficult months ahead we are all united in our dedication to bring about a lasting world peace."

Onto the election platform, the Republicans had nailed a plank promising statehood for the territories of Alaska and Hawaii; the two states-to-be were already knocking at the door of the Union. Frank visited Alaska several times as a member of the House Marine and Fisheries Committee and said,

"Alaska has a lot of potential wealth that must some day be developed. She might well become a protective bastion for the rest of America." (However, it would take until 1958 for Congress to vote for statehood for Alaska.)

After Frank's re-election, letters of congratulations and support for his message of unity came pouring in. The first one below was written on July 27, 1954, by Harry S. Truman (from the Federal Reserve Bank Building in Kansas City 6, Missouri):

Honorable Frank W. Boykin
House of Representatives
Washington, D.C.

Dear Frank:
I don't know when I received a letter that I appreciated more than I did yours of the seventeenth.
It was certainly kind and thoughtful of you to write me as you did about Bennett Clark. I was always fond of him but never agreed with him politically.
Warmest regards to you and Mrs. Boykin and thanks for your prayers.

Sincerely yours,
Harry Truman

The following one was from no less a figure than FDR:

November 22, 1954
Honorable Frank W. Boykin
412 House Office Building
Washington D.C.

Dear Colleague:
Please accept my heartiest congratulations on your re-election to the Congress and my very best wishes for continued success in your legislative efforts.

I sincerely enjoyed serving with you in the House of Representatives and regret very much that I shall not be with you during the 84th Congress.
With warmest regards,

Sincerely Yours,
Franklin D. Roosevelt, Jr.

Such a succinct letter seemed to sum up most of the feelings toward Frank that came from Capitol Hill.

CHAPTER FIFTEEN

U.S. Role with China

In July1954, at MacArthur's invitation, Frank Boykin, along with a few other congressmen, went for a four-hour visit and luncheon with the esteemed general. By then, MacArthur was retired and living in his suite at the Waldorf Towers in New York. He and Frank were old friends.

The setting for Frank's visit with General MacArthur was in his spacious living room, the walls of which were adorned with mementos of his long, distinguished career. His youthful soldiering still lingered about him. The echoes of his "there is no substitute for victory" were still ringing across the nation. To his guests, he was so personable and vital, with his brilliant mind that was so sharp and focused.

In *Everything's Made for Love*, Edward Boykin wrote of the general:

> *Step by step he recalled the sequences of the final drama in the Far East that brought him to grips with the politicians at Washington. He discussed America's role in the Far East and her lost opportunity in Asia. He spoke a lot on the crime of letting China go Communistic. Time and again he returned to the power houses in Washington, who refused to let him use the military air power to destroy the danger that threatened China with communism and all of Asia (pages 155 – 157).*

In depth, and to great applause, MacArthur discussed his armies' strategy and leading them to shape the destiny of the great Asiatic nation he had conquered. He told in detail of the inspired amphibious assault in

Inchon that pushed back the Red Korean armies, the tragedy of denying arms and munitions to fight the rising power of China's Communists at the outset, and of demanding that Chiang give Mao's "agrarian reformers" a place in his government.

MacArthur's congressional guests would talk for months of their visit with him, and they never forgot it. They carried away the image of a soldier and patriot, with love of country above all else, who had the highest of morals. He was a man victimized by politicians who had been squashed by their attacks, until the last one.

Waiting to see MacArthur as he ushered his guests out was President Syngman Rhee, the man installed in the seat of power in the Republic of South Korea. "Goodbye again, Frank," said MacArthur with a strong handclasp as he took leave of his friend. "I say, your plan might have saved China."

Buried somewhere in the debris of America's dealings with pre-Formosa Nationalist China is the historically significant plan that was evolved by Frank Boykin's Chinese associates for rescuing China from the grip of Mao Tse Tung's Reds. It is a story that should be told. A former contemporary in the House, Jasper Bell of Missouri, wrote to Frank long afterwards and observed, *"Your plan came within a hair's breadth of saving China as an ally of the United States."*

Even before entering Congress, Frank and China's powerful Soong family were friends of long standing. Behind the Soong's lay generations that had labored to create stable, free government in the once Celestial Empire. Frank and the Soong's dated back some years to a meeting with a Chinese girl who came halfway around the world to Georgia to enroll in a college presided over by a close cousin of Frank's mother, Methodist Bishop Ainsworth. It was he who converted the young lady, Miss Soong, to Christianity. Through him, Frank met the new convert. She was the youngest of the Soong sisters, a trio celebrated throughout the Far East for their beauty and brilliance. One of them married Dr. Sun Yet Sen, first president of Nationalist China. A second became the wife of Dr. H. H. Kung, a financial wizard who once headed the Bank of China, as well as occupying the Ministry of Finance of the Republic. The third, who had journeyed to Georgia for an education, married a young soldier later known to the world as Generalissimo Chiang Kai-shek. Through the general's lady, Frank presently met her equally famous brothers, Drs. T.V. and T.L. Soong. During World War II, the Soong's, were reputed to be the richest men in the world, advanced twenty million dollars to a boatbuilder, Andrew Jackson Higgins, to enable him to build a shipyard, where they constructed a type of small vessel that became an important weapon for the United States Navy.

By the end of 1949, the fate of Nationalist China on the mainland had already been destroyed by the U.S. State Department. General Chiang Kai-shek had miraculously evacuated the army of half a million or more veterans across Formosa Strait to the island of the same name. Once everyone was there, he re-established the government of Nationalist China under the watchful eyes and fighter planes of the United States Seventh Fleet. Ninety percent of the American people are unaware of the background of the flight of the Free Chinese government to Formosa.

In 1945, President Truman had relieved General George Marshall as Chief of Staff at Washington and dispatched him to China to resolve the civil war between the Nationalists under Generalissimo Chiang and the Communist Chinese exhorted by Mao-Tse-Tung. Marshall's instructions from the State Department were to endeavor to unify China by insisting that Chiang combine with Mao's "Agrarian reformers" and admit them to the inner circles of the nationalist government. As concocted by the Far Eastern Section of the State Department, Marshall's instructions proved the death warrant of Nationalist China on the mainland. Mystery still shrouds the actual author of these instructions.

Chiang refused to comply with the State Department's insistence on setting up a coalition government with the Chinese Reds. On Chiang's refusal, General Marshall promptly declared an embargo on all munitions of war for both sides. This was no hardship on the Communists. The Soviets were already pouring arms, munitions, artillery, aircraft and even transport trucks into their ranks. To top it all off, President Truman issued an order forbidding the sale of any American surplus weapons, "which would be used to fight a civil war." Chiang was left with little to carry on his successful war against Mao's regime.

General Marshall returned to Washington to be showered with jubilation. It was believed he had settled everything in China when he had settled nothing except Nationalist China. As a reward, he was elevated to secretary of state.

On December 5, 1950, Marshall received a long-distance phone call from the Honorable Sidney W. Souers: His reasoning was from the latest developments in Korea, as well as the events in Europe since 1945, the Communist realized that the gospel according to Saint Lenin stated that democracies and Communism could not co-exist. This was taken very seriously by the Communist regime. They vowed that with either democracies or Communism, one must go. He also realized that the Chinese Communists were not a bunch of "Agrarian reformers," but were the stooges of Soviet Russia, who released thirty G.I.s with good treatment one day, and on the next day, after the victory, doused gasoline over our wounded boys and burned them.

The following sentiments were written in a letter by the Honorable Frank W. Boykin, sent as 'personal' to Admiral Souers:

> *A crisis has come to the Country, the like of which had never been experienced. Ye ought to think objectively and from an overall picture of what we should do around the world, if we are to come out of it alive. They talk of a deal with the Chinese Communists, whereby in giving them recognition in the United Nations they would permit us to keep South Korea. That is reward for aggression. Why should we submit to this humiliation of being permitted to retain South Korea and give an equal voice in the Security Council of the United Nations to the Chinese aggressors?*
>
> *If we can keep South Korea by our own strength without too much cost, well and good; but if necessary, let us give it up for the time being. There is no disgrace in it, there is no loss of prestige. It is a display not of weakness, but of strength, and firmness of purpose. We are going to fight the enemy, not at his most convenient spot, but to fight him where we are superior. During the last war under the force of enemy local superiority we gave up the Philippines, didn't we? But we got it back, and that's what counts.*
>
> *Why do we pull out of Korea? It is in order to strengthen our outer ramparts, Japan, Okinawa, Formosa and the*

Philippine, didn't we? If we were to give up any of this chain of Islands, we would lose our outer bastions and fall back on a defensive warfare basing on the Continental United States with Hawaii as an Outpost. In addition, there is one highly important consideration for the coming long, drawn-out struggle in Russia and China the Soviet bloc has the manpower of Poland, Czechoslovakia, Hungary, Romania and Bulgaria.

In addition to our own strength there are two fighting stocks we could draw upon, the Germans and the Japanese. The Chinese masses have been overrun by the Communists. We shall eventually have them on our side, but only later.

We want Western Europe because we want their industrial potentials, and we want the manpower of Germany. We want to do everything we can to protect Western Europe and have it on our side. There is every reason why we should strengthen our European defenses. But we shall do it with our eyes open. We shall have as our allies, France which is Communists ridden, and an Ally whose chief of General Staff last year betrayed her to the Indo-China Communists. We have twenty five percent of the population their Communists.

We have a France which shortsightedly refused to recognize the real present danger of Soviet Russia and is afraid of the bogey of future German strength. We have Italy whose industrial population is largely Communist. Defend Western Europe we must, but we can have no illusions; it is not going to be an easy task with France and Italy as they are, and with the rest of the potential Allies such as they are. We must not be blind to the fact that despite everything we do, we might have to lose Western Europe.

But on the other side of the world with our superiority in the Air and in the Sea and with undying hatred of the Japanese against the Russians, our task of holding our Western Bastions would be easy. Bring every one of our G.I.s now in Korea into Germany and they may not be able to count against the one hundred and seventy-five Russian Divisions besides their satellite strength. But let these men go to Japan, under the cover of our sea power and air power, we can hold Japan, Okinawa, Formosa and the Philippines inviolate.

From now on we shall arm and arm to the teeth, and when we are thoroughly ready, we can choose our own Theatre of Operations, just as our enemy has chosen it this time. In the meantime, from our Pacific ramparts, we can strike back at the Chinese Communists by guerilla warfare, by sabotage, and if necessary, by air bombing and by blockade to keep them from consolidation, until we are strong enough to move either in Europe or on the mainland of Asia.

We will not recognize the Chinese Communists in the United Nations. It would be better if the United Nations were dissolved rather than to have aggression rewarded. When the Japanese conquered Manchuria in 1932 we steadfastly held on to the principle of non-recognition of aggression. We were not strong enough to fight Japan then, at least we were not ready, but we upheld the moral law which is the basis of our democratic society and in the end, we prevailed.

Let us be done with illusions, let us find the lowest common denominator of our strength and build from there on. Only thus we can expect the United States, and with it the hope of Democracy the World over.

From the White House, on December 8, 1950, came this response to his impassioned letter:

Honorable Frank W. Boykin
House of Representatives
Washington, D.C.

Dear Frank:
Sid Souers handed me your letter to him December fifth, I read it with a great deal of interest and appreciate very much you're expressing the opinions which you expressed to Sid.
Sincerely yours,
Harry Truman

A response to Congressman Boykin was also written from the General Headquarters' supreme commander for the Allied Powers (Office of the Supreme Commander, Tokyo, Japan) on December 13:

> *Apart from the controversial aspects of the late President Franklin D. Roosevelt's views, there was one public pronouncement he made, I believe during the Depression, which received universal accord: "The only thing we have to fear is fear itself." This expression holds as true today as it did then. Fear in the public mind is the primary objective of Communist propaganda methods in the so-called "cold war," unfortunately receiving strong support from the tendency toward sensationalism in our public press. This is not dishonestly inspired, but it has a profound influence upon the thinking of our people and often engender fear when the need for caution may be indicated, but reason for fear is non-existent. Thus I am informed that our recent action in the Korean campaign has been widely reported by such extravagant superlatives as 'decimated divisions,' 'military debacle' and such nonsense. In the absence of any political intelligence giving us the intentions of Communist China and the limitations upon effective air reconnaissance, our attack or reconnaissance in force, as it turned out to be, of the 24th became our only available means of securing adequate field intelligence upon which to estimate enemy strength and intentions. It prematurely brought to light and unbalanced the Chinese surreptitious build-up operations and provided us with conclusive intelligence on Chinese Communist intentions at a relatively low cost. The sensational reporting of our withdrawal movements from this action have produced a fear psychology which is just what the Kremlin would most desire. It is one of the less desirable consequences of a free press, but despite the harm it occasionally produces the free press must be preserved.*
>
> *Amid the confused thinking which seems so generally prevalent, it is refreshing indeed to read your calm and analytical viewpoint. Many of the words were powerfully written and stated by General Douglas MacArthur.*

Earlier in 1950, the Soong brothers appeared in Washington with a project for snaring China from the Reds. They went directly to Frank's office on

Capitol Hill, where they revealed a fully elaborated and documented plan for freeing China and perhaps saving the rest of Southeast Asia from ultimate engulfment by Communism. The strategy and logistics were integrated in detail. They submitted lists of former generals and field officers of the Nationalist China Army ready to fall in with the plan the moment the trigger was pulled. It was obvious they were able to deliver to the Allies two and a half million Chinese fighting men, as well as units of Mao's forces who were ready to abandon the red ranks. Undercover visits to the mainland had confirmed their estimates. The Soong's brought credentials and the blessings and cooperation of Generalissimo Chiang Kai-shek.

Frank consulted with Speaker Sam Rayburn, who enthusiastically told him to submit the plan to Carl Vinson, chairman of the House Armed Services Committee. Carl dashed cold water on the idea.

Boykin proceeded to present the idea to others and finally got to the secretary of Defense at the Pentagon. Now, Johnson was feuding with Secretary of State Acheson over the Far Eastern policy. He was sharp in his criticism of the policy that had helped Mao's "Agrarian reformers" take over China. Now he listened eagerly to the Soongs' proposals. He said, "Frank, I think the plan might work. It won't be necessary for you to do anything more. Don't resign from Congress as you suggest. I'll contact General MacArthur and put the operation in his hands and have him go see General Chiang."

For a month Johnson called Frank with a progress report. Then, in 1950, the Korean misadventure exploded with violence that rocked the entire Far East. One morning at dawn, Korean troops in great strength struck across the 38th Parallel, the agreed-online of demarcation between Communist North Korea and the South Korean Republic. The Red breakthrough was driving southward, sweeping aside all opposition with speed and power and lunging towards the capital city of Seoul. At the same time Red Chinese soldiers by the thousands, equipped with Russian tanks, artillery, small arms and planes, were poised on the Manchurian border along the Yellow River, ready to cross and join the Red Korean deluge flowing into South Korea.

General MacArthur's sphere of command was quickly re-activated, and he was ordered to retrieve the Korean disaster as best he could. The Red-oriented front of the State Department had, two years before, finagled the Korean Republic out of MacArthur's command and ordered withdrawal of his last troops from Korea.

In July 1950, General MacArthur flew to Formosa to visit General Chiang Kai-shek. There is no record of his having discussed the Soongs' plan with Chiang, though unquestionably it must have been done. It was during the visit that Chiang offered to send National Chinese troops to join Allies in Korea, but MacArthur felt such a move might jeopardize the defense of Formosa.

The Soong plan was blasted in the uproar and smoke of the Korean War. The United States had its hands full, and Defense Secretary Louis Johnson found himself bitterly assailed for the nation's inability to muster decisive forces quickly enough to cope with the Red Korean deluge flooding South Korea.

MacArthur brought the red tide to a halt. His "reward" came in April 1951, when President Truman was apparently pressured by the State Department "strategists" to retire General MacArthur from command in the Far East. Frank said, "If Harry Truman had not fired General MacArthur, I believe we would have rescued China from the Communists. It was a great tragedy. It was the only thing Truman ever did on which I disagreed with him wholeheartedly."

There were strong arguments in favor of the contention that, as president and commander-in-chief of a nation committed to cooperation with other members of the United Nations in a definite Far Eastern policy aimed at combating Communist aggression, Harry Truman had only one alternative to relieving General Douglas MacArthur of his command when it became evident that military groups were determined to promote a different course of action.

That alternative was repudiated by the U.N. policy of participating in the Korea crisis for the purpose of fulfilling pledges to that country to resist aggression and acceptance of the MacArthur thesis. His thesis included carrying the war directly to China by bombing raids and assisting the Nationalist forces of General Chiang Kai-shek to invade the mainland from Formosa for the purpose of diversionary action against the Communist forces of General Mao.

The repudiation sounded the death for the coalition of Western nations organized to present a united front against Communist aggression, leaving the United States to carry the burden of the campaign and wrecking hopes for achievement of a solid defensive line in Western Europe.

Many were ready to support any move that would place the nation upon a sane basis of readiness to act—even if it extended to the removal of President Truman, that worn-out political hack, Vice President Alben Barkley, Secretary of State Acheson and all of the examples of ineptitude that cluttered the Washington scene, who spent most of their time advocating socialism or stooging for the Truman gang.

Frank received hundreds of letters from his constituents in Alabama and people from other states protesting General MacArthur's firing by Truman. Many of the letters and telegrams read like this: "The last pillar of resistance to the spread of Communism has been removed from the Far East. MacArthur should be restored to his command in that theatre of operation, and the President and Dean Atcheson should be removed."

Others wrote: "All of my friends and everyone I have heard express an opinion, are with MacArthur 100 percent."

"MacArthur for president, and do it now," was shouted by Alabama and many other states.

Many agreed:

> *In the first place we are at war whether we admit it or not. Our men are getting wounded and killed and we cannot call this just policing. It is war, declared or undeclared. Who do we try to escape the fact and keep putting the inevitable off? The government is allowing our loved ones to be slaughtered for no good reason. Firing our great leader, who is trying to stop the fighting, instead of egging it on, by saying, 'It is not war.'*
>
> *With spouses overseas, some in the Naval reserves—which the dictionary meaning is a group trained to help the regular Navy in time of War—families with brothers in the Army who are risking their lives on the Korean Battle front, if it is not war*

why is such haste to ship men over? We know the threat of war is great. We will always be preparing for it and so will other nations such as Russia. No peace treaty is strong enough to be written to avoid War. There is too much greed and selfishness in this world. The word of God must be.

Rather a Christian or not or of age to vote, but a citizen of the United States and mother to be should have as much right as any other citizen to protest and give an opinion on the firing of MacArthur. People of all walks of life are for MacArthur!

Surely the uppermost wish in all our hearts is "peace." Maybe, the General was not right for his positions for Commander. He should have tried to agree with our Allies and President. There he was with his hands tied behind him, not able to do what he thought was best for our boys and his country. It must have been terrible, having to sit there while nothing but meetings and vacations went on in Congress with nothing being done about the men dying. Many citizens would take charge and leadership and help those overseas. MacArthur tried to bring about the end of War and destruction and could not get the help on the matter he needed back home; he got interference instead. He is beyond reproach except for a mistake, which the President has had many more and who seems to be in delight in insulting our fighting Forces, the Marines and anyone else, when it strikes his fancy. Who do we get to judge our President? The President passes judgment on innocent people as well as the Army Leaders. Many are of the old-fashioned belief the Government should be run by the people and not for the people and not by one person, which seems to be an old-fashioned belief because it is not carried out as it should be. We need to have Truman fired!

Is this what our fine beloved Country is coming to? That our forefathers fought for? That we all are equal. That one man may rule our Golden Country. He sends our men overseas on his own and he fires whom he pleases and writes whom he pleases. Yet, we the American people are supposed to sit back and look upon him with awe and respect. Many of us protest! This one-man kingdom has gone far enough.

The one person trying to stop the war was fired. We need MacArthur, who is a great leader! There are a lot of indignant citizens, which continues till this day.

Cries call out what a stupid blunder of getting rid of General MacArthur, and perhaps the greatest blunder in history. Some of this stupidity is chargeable to our Senators and Congressman, for they have allowed him to run with a free rein, particularly on the phase of sending our boys to Korea to be shot and killed with no aims of what our intentions are other than to play into the hands of England, France and Communism.

Get behind the movement to return General MacArthur to the States where the American people can get the facts first-hand and not get them piecemeal as handed out by our Administration leaders as they are always using subterfuge and half-truths to keep the American people from finding out they are being led down the road to chaos.

It makes our blood boil seeing American boys slaughtered. Day by day they continue cashing the taxpayer's dollar after dollar to no avail, nothing is accomplished!

Men and women wrote letters and even poetry to the Alabama congressman. The following was written by Tommie Little and sent to Frank Boykin:

Dear Congressman:

It's been said, "By their deeds you shall know them." That goes for the Russians, for H.S.T. and General MacArthur.

Need we have more to let us know what the Russians are up to.

Need we be made impotent by Truman's sugar-coated phrases.

Before we rise and defend ourselves.

Need MacArthur show more, than he has that he is a real General. He's like the prize fighter coming off the floor to score a knockout.

We all know that there can't be any division of command, but a wise president would take council with his general who has spent one fifth of his life in the Orient. Rather that of some of the Cream Puff Diplomats.

If the Alabama representatives are representing the people and not the administration, they won't wait for a bomb shell to burst before they act on this miscarriage of fair play against a real man and General.

I have a stake in this war as a taxpayer, one member in another about to leave and if it lasts long enough the third member of the family will be there.

If the British, French think by appeasing the reds, the colonial position will be status quo they have another guess. For in the end the white man will be driven out of Asia. In the prize fight ring, the only time the opponent was afraid was when I attacked. On one occasion I saw a 205-pound man go down on the onslaughts of a 165-pound fighter. If the lighter fellow had waited the heavier opponent would have caught him any place in the ring. And it goes the same anywhere else.

Andrew Edington, president of the Schreiner Institute in Kerrville, Texas, sent a brief note to the Honorable Frank Boykin: "*The entire state of Texas is highly indignant over the firing of General MacArthur. All is hoping Congress will express for the nation its disapproval in the strongest possible way. People are aroused.*" Frank Sturm, president of Personal Loan and Finance Corporation, wrote: "*It was the consensus of many businessmen that steps should be introduced at once to impeach President Truman. Recent investigations have brought to light ample grounds to justify such steps. Many people guarantee to secure the signatures of at least 1,000 businessmen and labor leaders. All being citizens in high repute.*"

People born in President Truman's home state of Missouri were disgruntled and expressed the following views:

> *If he retained the humility and sincerity that he showed when he became President, I would have still had great hopes, but he has evidently listened to wrong advisors that have not been familiar with dialectical mendacity, so as to avoid the pitfalls, consequently we lost China.*
>
> *All the blunders led up to General MacArthur's drastic dismissal and thus "confusion worse confounded" confronts our Nation.*
>
> *What are you as our representatives going to do to help straighten out this mess? Don't hide behind the worn phrase of the "President's constitutional rights." Stand for what you know is morally right and help our great country to overcome this confusion by earnestly seeking God's guidance. We are in a War up to the hilt and our men in Korea must be supported to win it. Listen to the people more and act to help them overcome their distrust of present leadership by standing boldly for the right regardless of power politics.*
>
> *The Christian people of the U.S. are praying for better leadership.*

On April 19, 1951, George Faulk, Jr. of Johnson Bible College wrote the following (slightly paraphrased):

> *The MacArthur incident has people doing a great deal of thinking. We have heard Rear Admiral Thornton C. Miller, who had just returned from Japan. Admiral Miller is a graduate of this school and a man in whom many have a great deal of confidence. He knows General MacArthur personally and told of the great work which he was doing in Japan. Admiral Miller, being a chaplain, was interested in MacArthur's work from a Christian viewpoint; I assure you that he respected and spoke highly of his Christian and humanitarian ideals. Having read of MacArthur and hearing of his work from other sources in Japan, most agree with Admiral Miller. The conviction as to the outstanding ability and character of MacArthur was further strengthened when his speech was said. MacArthur*

> is not partisan in politics. I vote for whom to the best of my knowledge is the best man.
>
> MacArthur spoke of the progress of Japan in the economic, political and democratic fields. Modest as he is, what he did not say was that a great deal of this progress is due to MacArthur himself. MacArthur said that nothing could be farther from the truth than that he was a war monger. Admiral Miller corroborated this statement before MacArthur spoke. He said that MacArthur said to him personally that he detested war. Admiral Miller spoke how MacArthur was a humanitarian to the Japanese people. MacArthur said in his speech that the problem of the World is basically theological and that if we are to save the flesh we must be of the spirit. I suggest that you write to any of the missionaries of any denomination in Japan and ask them what they think of MacArthur.
>
> He also said that if it is forced upon us every means must be applied to bring it to a swift end. Appeasement begets but a worse and bloodier war.
>
> Did not Chamberlain learn this sad fact when he tried to deal with Hitler? The only two appeasements are: (1) to avoid an all-out war with Red China. (2) to avoid Soviet intervention. Of course, no sensible man wants to send a full army of invasion into the Chinese mainland, but why not bomb the strategic points? China has already been termed an aggressor. Soviet intervention is inevitably coming, and no one with any political sense at all will deny. Decisive action should be taken, for a continued war of attrition is foolish.

David Lawrence wrote the following in the *Washington Scene* on April 19, 1951:

> Thus 60,000 casualties will have been suffered by the American government just to maintain the 38th Parallel and to admit that the UN could not push the aggressor out of Korea but must let him stay where he started from last June—ready, perhaps to jump across the parallel at any time. The Red Chinese have

said all foreign troops must be withdrawn and this presumably means the Communist North Koreans of course will remain. That's the appeasement plan. It will of course be denied that this is appeasement. But this was what was planned before General MacArthur was fired. Maybe it will not materialize now because American public opinion may prevent it from being consummated.

His political ideas are not always right but in this instance his point is well taken.

The last words of the Korean people to MacArthur before he left were "don't scuttle the Pacific." Many said let's "don't scuttle the Pacific."

MacArthur said that old soldiers just fade out and that is what he did when he said goodbye. Many cried out not to let him fade out like that, America needs him too much.

All party differences should be set aside and work together. We have nothing against Truman as a man, but as a President he has made a rotten job of it and has disgraced our country. This is just the consummation of a long series of political blunders. It is the worst of political crimes in the history of the United States. It is worse than the Tea Pot Dome scandal or the "Billy" Mitchell affair. The time has come for action. There are millions of people that want to impeach Truman not as a matter of partisan politics, but as a matter of general incompetency. Then offer to reinstate MacArthur. It is time for tyranny to end in a democratic America.

Many Americans were great admirers of the general, especially those who were students of his life's work since he attended West Point Academy. He was perhaps the greatest combination of statesman, diplomat and military leader of his generation and ranks a place in the Hall of Fame alongside Winston Churchill.

Some dramatic thoughts were written that the discharge of General MacArthur, one of America's greatest generals, by a man who had been a complete failure in everything he had done, and was establishing a record as the worst president in America's history, was the greatest break that Stalin had ever had and was, in fact, Stalin's finest victory:

> *How can one stomach the terrible conditions that now prevail in the administration at Washington? The dishonesty, corruption, and the low moral character of the group that surrounds the President are constantly being exposed.*
>
> *This country must be saved from this group of socialist planners, if necessary, by impeachment of President Truman, who has shown no inclination to discharge any of the corrupt members of his official family and will not turn his back on the man who refused to turn his back on a convicted traitor of his country. Many felt to avoid disintegration of our Far Eastern policy is to remove appeaser Atcheson.*
>
> *Atcheson and his socialist cronies in Britain are having one of their happiest moments over the discharge of General MacArthur. It's a pity that a President of our great country has to be told what to do by a group of socialists in Britain who are unwilling to carry more than 5 percent of the load of the Truman war in Korea.*
>
> *There were many differences of opinion on General MacArthur's actions, but General MacArthur is a soldier and wants to save the lives of soldiers who fight under his command and when he sees the incompetents in Washington taking their leads from Britain and with no coherent plan of actions at all but to create a stalemate, regardless of the loss of lives of our boys, he desires action that he believes in winning the war quickly and saving lives that will be needlessly sacrificed to the political desires of the Washington clique of appeasers and British socialists that are vainly protecting their holdings in Hong Kong, regardless of the sacrificing of American soldiers' lives.*
>
> *General MacArthur has the courage to speak out in the face of attacks of administration hatchet man and our so-called friends in England who want only to delay action so they can*

appease the communists in hopes that everything will work out by itself.

A rather strong letter was written to the Honorable Frank W. Boykin:

*House Office Building
Washington, D.C.*

Dear Congressman:

The uncouth way the President used to throw General MacArthur out indicates that he is totally unfit to occupy the exalted office of President of the United States. Further, he is unqualified to lead this Nation during times of peace—God only knows where he would take us in times of crisis without some reins being placed on him by the Congress of the United States. We further interpret his action as playing into the hands of both Communist China and Russia. We note that England and France now want to give Formosa to Communist China.

We request that you immediately get behind the movement to bring General MacArthur back to the Unites States so that he can inform the American people of the policies which are being formulated by the present administration which is leading this Nation down the path to chaos not only from military standout but also leading us into bankruptcy which in turn will deliver this Nation, the greatest Nation on the face of the earth, into the hands of the Communist without their firing a single shot.

Further the Administration's policy of giving to every Nation that stretches out their hands is a fallacy, for those Nations which we have befriended and put back on their feet are now ready and eager to stab us in the back.

We definitely feel that Tax and Spend and Give should come to an end and also a plan developed whereby we will know what our aims are in Korea.

*Yours truly,
L.W. Croy*

Perhaps the most direct and to-the-point letter was from H. L. Hunt of Dallas, Texas, sent to Congressman Frank Boykin on April 18, 1951:

Dear Mr. Boykin:

The wave of indignation caused by the ousting of General MacArthur should be controlled and directed into channels which will result in some good and offset to some extent the terrible loss.

1. *This must not be permitted to become a partisan affair which would result in the majority unduly condemning General MacArthur for any mistakes which he has made and glossing over the misconduct and mistakes of the State Department.*
2. *It is not in anywise a partisan issue because the State Department would have been the same should the Republicans have elected in '48 except that John Foster Dulles would probably be Secretary of State instead of Acheson. Dulles sees eye-to-eye with Acheson.*
3. *The public clamor offers a wonderful opportunity to call to account those who were instrumental in the giving way of China, the setting up of the 38th Parallel boundary line, Berlin and other situations which were arranged for the benefit of the Communists and to serve to our great disadvantage.*
4. *It would be a mistake for us to deal with personalities rather than fundamentals. The aroused public opinion should be directed toward cleaning up the State Department and not necessarily to eulogizing General MacArthur, to whose prestige nothing can be added.*
5. *Should there be stronger men than Acheson, Dulles, Jessup and Lattimore who direct their utterances and actions, they must be uncovered, exposed and held accountable. Perhaps Alger Hiss was a stronger and more adroit man than any of them but it is not likely that he is so influential in his present situation.*

6. In addition to cleaning up the personnel in the State Department the present situation could be used to arrive at a workable Asiatic policy and, in fact, a more sensible complete foreign policy.
7. MacArthur held Japan completely free from Communism during the time that the State Department surrendered country after country into Communism. Japan must not now be permitted to go the way of these other nations. There may be danger that the peace plan which Dulles is working on will be consummated in such a way that Japan would be left in charge of and at the mercy of Russia.
8. Formosa must never be turned over to a Red China. Red China must not be admitted to the United Nations.
9. If we are to continue to fight Asiatic on the ground, we must have Asiatic allies who will do a large part of such fighting. Perhaps the Nationalist Chinese would fight effectively on our side and certainly the Japanese could be expected to.
10. If Japan is not permitted to rearm whereby, they can carry on commerce with the Asiatic mainland their 82 million population will become an intolerable burden on us.
11. Any kind of a stalemate in Korea which leaves a part of Korea, Japan and the Philippines dependent upon us to maintain their countries in the face of the Communistic threat will become such a burden as to ultimately force us to abandon all the Far East. We cannot carry on in the Far East unless we have self-sustaining friends in force who are dependable.
12. Above all else, the American soldier must be able to feel quite sure that our State Department is on his side.

The public is aroused to a point whereby it may be possible to correct many situations which, if uncorrected, will surely lead to destruction.

I hope that some of the points which I have raised or suggestions which I have made can be useful.
With best wishes,

Constructively,
H.L. Hunt.

(Such are the similar sentiments felt today over what is going on with the Iraq War and Korean nuclear development.)

Congressman Frank Boykin received telegrams and mail every day from people of all walks of life. He would respond to each letter received; of the hundreds of thousands, most were from Alabama, but many came from across the country. Many Boykin's responses to MacArthur's firing said something similar to the following:

As you doubtless know, I am a very strong admirer of General MacArthur and I personally felt that the plan to utilize Chinese Nationalist troops and save our own boys was a good one. We expect General Macarthur in Washington Thursday, at which time we expect to have a thorough airing of this entire situation and a clarification of our Far Eastern policy.

I want you to know how much I appreciate your writing me, and you may rest assured that as one member of Congress, I intend to take such action as I feel will be to our country's best interest.

Below is General MacArthur's address at Norfolk, Virginia, when the dedication of the memorial to his mother, Mary Pinckney Hardy, on November 18, 1951:

With a sense of deep humility and reverence, I join you today as the son of that gentlewoman of Virginia whose memory you honor by this beautiful memorial at the hallowed site of her birth. I bring with me an inadequacy of words to describe the emotions which fill my heart.

In those troubled days when our country was engaged in civil strife, this Lovely Lady and her family were dedicated to the cause of the Confederacy. From this spot Hardy's followed "Marse Robert's" flag on Virginia's bloody fields and a Hardy was at "Old Jack's" elbow that dark night when he fell on the sodden Plank Road near Chancellorsville. The rebel yell and the sound of "Dixie" have been in my ears since birth.

My father was of the North—one of the most gallant soldiers who wore the Blue. Their marriage of deepest love and devotion came at the close of that mighty struggle between differing ideas but equally honest convictions. It seemed almost prophetic, as a prelude to the spiritual union which was later to unite again the North and South.

I am truly a mixture of the Blue and Gray, a living symbol of that united America which largely resulted from the nobility and deep spirituality which mothers of both South and North brought to the welding of a new union between the States. Sons of both have been molded into an invincible comradeship through common heritage of freedom. Thus, have been brought to fruition my mother's and my Father's dreams and hopes sanctified at the altar of holy matrimony, even as the smoke and stench and anguish of the aftermath of battle still hung heavily over the hearts of men.

It was my sainted Mother who first taught me of the gentle culture of the South and of its long and noble traditions and who infused in me a deep and lasting veneration for them which is indelibly etched upon my heart. She taught me, too, a devotion to God and a love of country which have ever sustained me in my many lonely and bitter moments of decision in distant and hostile lands. To her, at this shrine of memory, I can but yield anew a son's reverent thanks for her guidance to a path of duty as God gave me the light to see that duty.

I know how deeply stirred would "Pinky" Hardy be today could she look down upon this mark of honor and affection by her neighbors and her neighbor's children and children's children. And in her behalf and for all of her blood, I offer you my heartfelt gratitude.

The address shows the heart and dignity MacArthur had as a leader and a man. It is no wonder, then, that he and Frank Boykin became friends.

From the Seminole Wars to the Battle of Atlanta

By FRANK ROWSEY

A FIRST hand account of a little known but nevertheless important campaign against the Seminole Indians in South Georgia is contained in the diary of John Banks, a prominent merchant and planter, who was born in Elbert County in 1797 and died at his home in Columbus in 1870.

This remarkable document which has only recently come to light is now in the possession of Mrs. M. J. Leonard of Austell, a granddaughter. The author himself describes his writing as a "laconic biographical sketch of myself," with other incidental remarks"—but one glance at the manuscript is enough to show that John Banks, who became one of the wealthiest men in Middle Georgia, had reflected vividly, if sporadically, nearly three quarters of a century of Georgia history—a history in which he participated. For at eighteen years of age we find him fighting hostile Indians in Southwest Georgia. Toward the middle of his life we find the state's industrial growth mirrored in the many enterprises which he controlled. And later, as an old and broken man, one finds him with seven sons in the armies of the Confederacy, mourning the three who were never to return.

For a few years after the close of the War of 1812 the Creek Indians of South Georgia remained comparatively quiet. But such quiet was not for long. John Banks, keeping a store for his brother-in-law in Elberton as a young man of twenty years, "listened with envy to the stories of the soldiers on their return from the British and Indian wars of 1812, '13 and '14." So in 1818 when the Seminole Indians in East Florida "committed repeated murders and depradations on the Georgia frontier which brought on an Indian war," John Banks determined to try a campaign himself just as soon as the opportunity came.

Elected a first lieutenant in one of the two companies drawn from Elbert County, Banks and his men set out for the war, going to Lexington and then to Milledgeville where, the young recruit records, "I saw for the first time General Jackson, later the president, who took command of the army."

The departure from Milledgeville was a hurried one and the spring of 1818 was none too pleasant for campaigning. "We marched about eight miles that night, very cold, had much snow to wade through. On the 20th (February, 1818) we reached the fort (Fort Early on Flint River, twelve miles south of the present town of Cordele). From Hartford to this place we had an pleasant march of it. The distance is only 48 miles which took us eight days hard march. It rained nearly all the time, the waters were very high, we had to build some bridges and flats to cross the creeks on. We carried our baggage wagons till we got in ten miles of the fort, found it impractical to carry them any farther. They were dismissed and we took our provisions on our backs, officers and all, and performed the balance of the expedition without a wagon. We suffered considerably for provisions before we reached the fort, for our flour gave out and left us nothing but pork. We crossed the Flint River four miles below the fort. We had a rough

Mrs. Franklin D. Roosevelt, who was the central figure at a press conference in Birmingham attended by a large group of newspaper men, college journalists, photographers, radio folk and others, is shown in the above picture, taken during the conference at Tutwiler Hotel . . . With Mrs. Roosevelt are Representative Frank W. Boykin, Mobile, and Mrs. Boykin.

INN DIXIE   December, 1939   Page 5

CHAPTER SIXTEEN

Fabulous Frank

In 1954, energetic Frank was seeking his twelfth term in the House of Representatives. He was in trouble politically, or so it appeared to the pundits of the press. John Mandeville was his formidable opponent. The editor of a small weekly, *The Tallahassee Tribune*, wrote a piece at this time that no doubt expressed the sentiments of hundreds of Alabamians:

FABULOUS FRANK

We would as soon miss seeing the Capitol, White House and Washington Monument as we would miss seeing Frank Boykin on a visit to Washington.

The fabulous representative from the First District is Alabama's congressman at large. If for any reason he cannot secure something for his district he will work as hard to get it for one of his colleagues as he can.

Frank probably knows more people in Washington than any other person in the government service. And he probably entertains more people from other parts of the country than the average congressman does from his own district.

A human dynamo that lifted himself up by his own bootstraps, Frank was once called 'one of nature's noblemen.' To us that is a gross understatement.

With that we had the ability to write one of those 'unforgettable character' stories about the multi-jet Mobile man.

> *But you would probably not believe if it we had. You cannot read about Frank...you must see him in action to believe there is such a person.*

On a Sunday morning in May, shortly before the primaries, in a Mobile newspaper there was a political advertisement featuring a letter from Republican Speaker Joseph Martin, Jr. praising Frank's services in the House and calling for his reelection. Written on the speaker's official letterhead, the Martin letter was paired with a restrained telegram from Democratic leader Sam Rayburn, former majority leader, supporting Frank's nomination.

Under the bold headline, "THE NATION'S LEADERS ENDORSE FRANK BOYKIN AND READ WHAT THE LEADERS OF BOTH PARTIES IN THE U.S. HOUSE OF REPRESENTATIVES HAVE TO SAY ABOUT YOUR CONGRESSMAN," the two endorsements were spread across the newspaper page:

> *Dear Frank: I hope you will have no difficulties in your primary campaign. We, who are fighting for sound American government, need your re-election. The next two years are very important years for the American people, and we must have sturdy American champions like you here in Congress. With very best wishes, I am sincerely yours, Joseph W. Martin.*

On April 14, 1954, at 5:50 p.m., Sam Rayburn sent the following telegram:

> *I have your telegram; I never try to influence races in other states. But you have asked me for my estimate of Frank Boykin as a Congressman. I find Mr. Boykin a man very popular with his colleagues. Very industrious and he is a real influence in the House of Representatives. I have watched his work and it is not only splendid for his District but for the entire country. Sam Rayburn*

The political advertisement was paid for by John E. Polston, Chairman of the Boykin Campaign Committee in Mobile, Alabama, who stated that Sam Rayburn of Texas, speaker of the House of Representatives under two presidents and then the Democratic leader in Congress, and Joseph W. Martin, Jr. of Massachusetts, the current speaker of the House, were great Americans and two of the most influential men in the U.S. Rayburn served as speaker longer than any man in this country's entire history, and Martin was President Eisenhower's right-hand man in the House of Representatives. Rep. Rayburn was a Democrat, and Rep. Martin a Republican. But both had the confidence and the respect of the nation. He continued:

> *What these two outstanding leaders say about Frank Boykin must fill every thoughtful Alabamian with pride—for here is proof positive that the First District Congress is represented in Congress by a man who is loved and admired by his colleagues.*
>
> *Such praise cannot be purchased. SUCH PRAISE CAN ONLY BE EARNED BY LONG, UNSELFISH AND DISTINGUISHED DEVOTION TO DUTY. Note well that Speaker Martin calls Frank Boykin a sturdy champion of sound American government. Note too, that Sam Rayburn calls him a real influence in the House of Representatives, very industrious and a splendid worker not only for this District but for America.*
>
> *There can be only one conclusion—Frank Boykin is a truly outstanding Congressman. His re-election, endorsed by the two leaders of the two great American parties, is bound to benefit us all—and to reflect credit on all those voters who every two years have returned Frank Boykin to the House of Representatives.*

On primary day, the First District returned Frank to the House by a two-to-one vote, knowing that he truly voted his conscience as an independent.

CHAPTER SEVENTEEN

Affirmatives and Upheavals

In 1954, President Eisenhower's Tidelands Bill came up for a vote in the House and Frank lined up with the affirmatives. This measure, granted to the states to clear titles to their submerged lands and resources out to their historic boundaries, was the antithesis of Secretary Ickes' objectionable proposal in 1946 to rob the states of title to the coastal lands. The tidelands controversy was mainly between the United States and Texas and involved 2,440,650 acres of submerged land in the Gulf of Mexico.

Early in President Eisenhower's second term, tax-slashing bills were daily stuffing the hoppers in the House. Republicans and Democrats alike leaped into the tax cut act with bills to ease the excises on just about everything from graters to easy chairs for taxpayers. Joining the cutters' parade, Frank would release a bit of humor with his suggestion that automobile seat-covers be exempted from the taxes. To a member who took exception to his proposal, he replied, "They're necessities, aren't they? Don't they save a fellow's pants as well as the upholstery?"

National defense was also the theme of a dozen Boykin speeches during the 1950s, when the nation was building up its armament against the Russian nuclear threat. In 1954, Frank flew out to the atomic grounds in Nevada to witness the firing of the world's first atomic artillery shell. He returned to Washington impressed with the idea that America must have the ultimate in weapons for her defense should the cold war suddenly leap into flames. Two days after his return to Washington, he was on his feet, asking his colleagues, "Can a second-rate Air Force keep peace for America?"

Holding court, he stated:

> Mr. Speaker, the gift to see ourselves the way others see us is to furnish the United States defense, once a year, by the publication of a British reference book, Jane's Fighting Ships, the 1952 edition.
>
> In this authoritative guide I find the altogether encouraging and reassuring statement that the United States Navy 'is as large as all the navies of the world put together.' Certainly, against the threat of aggressive communism represented by Soviet Russia, Red China, and the satellites, it is important to have a Navy second to none. With a Navy as large as all the other navies of the world put together, we have a better chance of security, and for long survival of our American way of life.
>
> I am myself not at all sure that our great peacetime Navy is as strong in submarine as it ought to be. The Russian Navy amounted to very little in World War II, and as a surface navy it amounts to little more now. But Jane's says there are 370 Russian submarines in reserve or service, with 120 more being built. That is a total of almost 50 of two and a half times more than the number of United States submarines.
>
> The disconcerting thing about Jane's revelation of the size of our Navy was large as all the other navies of the world put together with the knowledge that we do not have an Air Force as large as Russia's. The NATO powers do not have air forces sufficient to compete with Russia's, even when they are all added together. Not too long ago the United States Air Force was the world's biggest. Today it is second rate and supported by third and fourth raters.
>
> Mr. Speaker, in two editorials in the Philadelphia Inquirer I found some interesting discussion of the biggest navy and the second-rate air force, as suggested by the publication of Jane's Fighting Ships.

> The writer said: "With the entire foreign policy of this country based on the idea of preserving peace through strength, the question Americans are asking is: Can a second-rate air force keep the peace? Particularly when our country is at war in Korea."
>
> The writer points out that the American people have been taxed for what they thought was to be a first-rate defense program. The writer asserts, and with him I am in wholehearted agreement, that the American people are entitled to satisfactory answers to their questions about the appropriated funds that have not been spent, the planes not yet built, the rate of our plane production as compared with the rate of Soviet production, and questions about our readiness to resist and defeat attack in another Korea.
>
> Mr. Speaker, we shall all look with eagerness for answers to these and other questions to be provided by the new Secretary of Treasurer of Defense, Mr. Wilson, and the new administration headed by President Eisenhower. In the words of the editorial: "We raise these questions not in any spirit of hostility. We seek information. For the question we are asking and we repeat this: Can a second-rate United States Air Force keep the peace?"

Admiral Rickover, whose biting remarks about America's naval deficiencies lifted him into the national spotlight, was a witness before the Merchant Marine and Fisheries Committee of the House one day when he suddenly interrupted the testimony. "Is this a proper thing to say publicly?" he inquired, giving an implied criticism of the Navy.

"It is all right," assured Congressman Herbert Bonner of North Carolina, committee chairman.

"Safe in here, perhaps," conceded admiral, "but I have to get out of here someday."

The city of Washington was also in a tense situation, filled with rumors about presidents and their first ladies. Every rumor was picked up by chatterers and magnified into 'truth.' No presidential couple was ever immune.

Rumors of Mrs. Eisenhower's impoliteness to visiting delegations, when previous administrations treated them like VIPs, were flourishing through the Hill. Unverified reports of Mrs. Eisenhower's health, habits, waste of time, card playing and varied shortcomings were widely spread in Washington. At the White House, she often failed to show up at luncheons and brunches given in her honor. Not all were in agreement with these assumptions and felt that the first lady was a great woman who was doing an outstanding job of supporting her husband.

* * *

To add to the stress was the matter of money. Legislatures were always cautious of raising their salaries, but not in 1955, when the members of the legislature on Capitol Hill gathered together enough courage to raise their pay from fifteen thousand dollars a year to twenty thousand and five hundred dollars, with a three-thousand-dollar allowance for income tax deductions. Supported by former president Truman, President Eisenhower and the House leaders of both parties, the statesmen beat back attacks on the motives of those sponsoring the pay raise bill.

The pay increase was long overdue, though political danger was always inherent in increasing one's own wages. Nobody but themselves could enlarge their pay, and voting for money for one's own pocket always draws criticism to the electorate.

In the 1870s, in response to President Grant's request, the Republican majority approved the "Salary Grab Bill," as it was dubbed. The measure included a provision making the pay boost retroactive to cover two preceding years so that each member of Congress might go home with an expected five thousand dollars in his pocket. In the same bill, the president's salary was doubled.

In the next Congressional elections, there was a Democratic landslide that quickly took control of the House from the Republicans for the first time since the Civil War. It was a political nightmare that posed frightening visions for future Congresses whenever mentions of more pay were even whispered.

As all this was going on, the president's heart was stricken while visiting Denver in September. Frank wrote him a letter, inviting him to

"God's country on Mobile Bay" for his convalescence. Promptly came the reply from Mamie Dowd Eisenhower:

Dear Mr. Boykin:

The President and I are deeply touched by your concern for his health and by your kind invitation to come to the Mobile Bay area; and I am sure that everything there is just as restful and beautiful as you say it is. The doctors feel, however, that we should go through with our present plan to go back to our home at Gettysburg as soon as the President is well enough to travel, because, in that setting, which means so much to both of us, he can get the rest his doctors prescribe and at the same time resume his official duties.

So many things in your letter are interesting to me and the President that I can't touch on them all. Just let me say both of us thank you so much for your interest and your thoughtful concern.

The second session of the Eighty-fourth Congress opened in January 1956, with battles over civil rights largely on its agenda; both Republicans and Northern Democrats were forcing the issue.

In March, nineteen senators and seventy-seven representatives from the old Confederate states signed and issued an anti-Supreme Court Manifesto that committed the signers to utilize every legal means of reversing the Supreme Court's ruling against segregation in favor of mixing the races. Many protested the Supreme Court ruling of 1954 as "unconstitutional" and "chaos creating abuse of judicial power." They labeled the document: "A Declaration of Constitutional Principles." Two Southerners, Senator Majority Leader Lyndon Johnson and Speaker Sam Rayburn, were not asked to sign because the signers did not wish it to appear as if the document represented national Democratic policy or the leaderships of both Houses of Congress. Among the seventy-seven signatures appended to the document was that of the president's two-time opponent, Adlai Stevenson.

The election proved that the people still liked Ike, though they were disturbed over world conditions, particularly the shootings in Hungary and Egypt. It also forecasted that the Negro vote would shortly rise to proportions that would give the white man in the South something to reckon with. Thanks to the black votes in Chicago and Baltimore, Ike carried Illinois and Maryland. (In November 1956, President Eisenhower would repeat his personal triumph at the polls with a second-term victory over Adlai Stevenson.)

In 1954, Earl Warren was chief justice of the United States and declared school integration. The race riots, integration marches, sit-ins and sit-downs in the South rated front-page headlines, but racial harmony and the promotion of it seldom received publicity in the North.

One morning, Frank Boykin received a letter postmarked "Boykin, Alabama." He had never heard of the place until receiving the letter. The town's one white man wrote it for his fellow black citizens. This was what he wrote:

> *This community is small and entirely colored, but we have hopes of expanding by education of the young folks and the guidance of the older people in better methods of farming...*
>
> *Being in public office you often have a thankless job. May this letter be just a token of appreciation for all the good things you have done for us.*

For several years Frank made substantial contributions to the blacks of the little settlement. He enabled them to get easy loans to build homes and buy small farms. His personal contributions to improve their school were considerable. To upgrade the breed of their scrubby livestock, he sent them a Brahma bull and a thoroughbred boar. Lastly, he persuaded the government to give them a post office. He helped many of these black citizens buy land in what is known as Gee's Bend in Alabama. He bought its river bottom land for $7.50 an acre. The government built them a post office and appointed the first black female postmistress.

The year before, an Alabama newspaper editor had on page one the story of a Negro who had for years driven a turpentine wagon on the Alabama plantation of his white employer. The worker was straightforward and dependable, and his employer knew that. Ten years before, the man had lost his eyesight and his working days were over. Each week, however, the white employer still sent him his weekly paycheck. His explanation was that the Negro labored for him long and hard. For many years that ex-worker received his money and lived in a small, rent-free home on Boykin's plantation in Washington County, Alabama. Frank had helped build homes for many whites, blacks and Indians alike, in his part of the country, who never dreamed of owning a roof over their heads.

All the NAACPs, Corps, marches to and fro, and vote-seeking on Capitol Hill could not have added more to this man's happiness. He had a home and a weekly income that he would have the rest of his life, even if the unforeseen of the Boykin empire went to pot. These stories add to the fact that the horrendous image of the Southern white man was largely painted by anti-Southern newspapers and broadcasters.

* * *

In May 1956, the First District of Alabama returned Frank to Congress for his eleventh term in the House. The trend in that year's primary in Alabama gave indications that this segment of the South was moving away from its Democratic solidity. Alabama turned Dixiecrat and was greatly influenced by the rising intensity of the racial issue. The storm that flared over the admittance of a black girl to the University of Alabama at Tuscaloosa, as well as the black boycott of segregated buses in Montgomery, had a tremendous backlash with many upheavals.

Still, Frank remained as popular as ever. On May 20, 1957, Dan Meininger from Davenport, Iowa, wrote the following letter:

> *Dear Representative Boykin,*
> *My name is Dan Meininger and I am fifteen years old. For some time, I have had a keen interest in good government and politics. I strongly feel it is my duty as an American youth to know and understand my government.*
> *To further my interest, I am making a scrapbook of famous men in government.*

For this reason, I would like very much to have a personally autographed picture of yourself plus a personally autographed letter.

I greatly appreciate your help in making my scrapbook. With best wishes, and again many thanks, I remain,

Yours sincerely,
Dan Meininger

The following excerpts are from a letter written on August 8, 1957 (dictated on August 7, 1957):

Mr. T.J. Rester
264 Cherokee Street
Mobile, Alabama

Dear Res:
Well, I hoped to be with you all today, but I can't leave this Black-Connery bill fight. I don't know if we are going to be able to beat it or not, but we have got it all torn to hell and Mr. Hugo won't know his bill when he does it. Of course, I am going to fight on to the last ditch to get it knocked out altogether, because we don't need it.

The naval store people, however, along with many other people, are exempt. We are going to keep on fighting, and I believe even if it is passed it will be unconstitutional. I don't know. Lee Robinson has certainly done a splendid job on this.

I have never worked quite as hard as I have, working day and night. But boy, we are busting them up, and if we never do anything else, I think we will at least rid Alabama of Hugo Black forever. Lord knows, he has been a pain, and has caused most of the trouble, with such things as the Supreme Court bill, the wages and hours bill, and every other darn kind of a bill that is impractical, unworkable, and everything else.

I will write you another letter a little later, because we are just snowed under, and my desk is piled high with telegrams, letters and everything else. We get a telegram about every five minutes, from all over Alabama, and about thirteen other Southern States.

I do hope that you and Mrs. Rester will go and see Ocllo as often as you possibly can, because I know she is lonesome. Keep me fully posted about everything.

With love to all of you, always, I am

Sincerely your old friend
Frank W. Boykin

Midyear 1957 found the North and South on Capitol Hill engaged in a relentless civil rights battle that was like a verbal lightning round. In a bitter speech, Senator Richard Russel, leader of the Southern Bloc in the Upper House, chastised President Eisenhower's civil rights bill as a forerunner of the House rule below the Potomac and a return to the Reconstruction era.

One day, at the height of the furor, Frank entered the House cloakroom to overhear a Republican member remark, "If we can pass this civil rights bill, we can snap up every Northern black vote and sweep the House of Representatives at the next election."

Frank said, "You Republicans have suddenly discovered that there's black gold in them their hills!"

In July, the House passed the civil rights bill and sent it on to the Senate, where it squeaked by on a compromise. It was the first realistic civil rights measure since the Reconstruction, but it was clear to Frank that the legislation was merely a way to pave for harsher measures aimed at the South.

The South during the Reconstruction was driven wholeheartedly into what was then the Democratic and Conservative Party; they were driven into it as the result of a disastrous Civil War. The despair of the South had set in over the bitterness and the vengeance of overzealous unionists, and some of the leading Republicans of the Lincoln administration bent all their energies toward its destruction. The Republican Party of that day had mellowed to a point where Southern Democrats recognized the existence of eminent statesmen with a spirit of fairness toward the South, and cooperation between Republicans and Southern Democrats in Congress began to take place. For example, the principle of Social

Security was considered one of the elements of progress, and the principle of reasonable help to other nations was defensible.

In 1951, the administration had been allowed temporary assistance from the general treasury and members saw to it that their section of the country got its full share of the assistance being offered—but the day had long since passed when any member of Congress was justified in scattering the people's tax money beyond reason. The cooperation of the two parties during that time was somewhat effective on this point.

There was also sound political wisdom in the argument by Congressman Clifford P. Case, but from the Southern point of view, he had an erroneous view of the situation in the South. He had too much to say about racial prejudice in the South, when it was not prejudice toward the black population but racial pride and a distinctive separation that has existed since the Tower of Babel. The North, South, East and West had the same racial pride and lived and acted upon it. But for him, it marked the end of the South as he had known it. Nor would it settle the issue that beleaguered the South and the nation for a century and a half, just as abolition did.

The following telegram was sent to President Eisenhower on Tuesday, July 23, 1957:

> *President Eisenhower, White House, Washington D.C.*
>
> *Please take time out from your golf to remember that white southern people have some Constitutional Rights as well as the minority whose votes are wanted by politicians. You are persecuting the South through your Thaddeus Stevens henchmen. We happen to be American citizens despite you or ourselves.*
>
> *Signed Miss. Mary A Gaillard*

Her sentiments reflected many of those in the South at that time. People would hear one day that the president did not want to call out troops in the South, and then he would ask for the bill. Understandably, the president's prestige was very low. Many were full of hate and resentment that the administration destroyed the greatest country in the world. The feelings were that they were not bettering the blacks but spreading hate and distrust.

Out of a clear sky one day, in September 1957, on President Eisenhower's orders, federal paratroopers descended on Little Rock, Arkansas, to integrate a high school at bayonet's point. Little Rock became a landmark in the South's struggle to hold on to what it considered its constitutional way of life. The event is still shrouded in mystery.

Shortly after the Little Rock incident, Frank called Sherman Adams, the president's right-hand man, and informed him that the president had lost face with thousands of friends in the South as a result of the confrontation.

* * *

In January 1958, Frank was a candidate for a thirteenth term in the House. He had no challenger to test the Boykin political lightning, being unopposed for re-election. But in that 'winter of discontent,' the Census Bureau at Washington said that as a result of the upcoming 1960 elections, it was probable that fourteen states, including Alabama, would lose seats in the House of Representatives.

The Census foretold of the mighty upheavals in Alabama's political hierarchy in Washington.

CHAPTER EIGHTEEN

Power Struggles

After Eisenhower's report to the nation on the Berlin crisis in March 1959, the president's words moved Frank to write the following:

Mr. President:

Truly you were fabulous. I don't believe in all the great speeches you have made that have covered this earth from end to end, you have ever made a better one. You looked so hale and hearty and sounded so wonderfully good, so sincere, and there certainly could be no misunderstanding where our President stood on backing up Berlin. Many years from now that talk, and that great television program will be played over and over.

I believe it will do lasting good and foresight and you were so forthright in that great talk that means and will mean so much to all mankind. God bless and keep you and give you strength to keep on keeping on in these uncertain, terrible times. God bless you again good. Sincerely, your friend,

Frank W. Boykin.

President Eisenhower responded in kind:

Dear Frank:

Thank you very much indeed for your message concerning my television talk of last Monday evening. I am truly grateful

for your comments, and I appreciate immensely your support in these days of tension. With warm regards, Sincerely,
Dwight D. Eisenhower.

The Democrats had once again retrieved control of the House they lost in 1952. But Eisenhower's eight-year tenure of the White House would elapse in January 1961. Historically, his mantle should have fallen on Vice President Richard Nixon, though as of then the incumbent had not committed himself. Nixon became the top spot on the Republican ticket.

Though there was political turmoil as usual, things seemed to be going smoothly for Frank at the time, as evidenced by the *Mobile Press Register* on February 3, 1958:

BOYKIN ENTHUSED ON SELECTION AS HONORARY ADMIRAL

Now it is "Admiral" Frank W. Boykin of the South Carolina Navy.

The Mobile Congressman has received a six-star admiral's cap from the Sumter Guards at Charleston, S.C. and his delight were so great that he sent the cap down to Mobile for his friends to admire. It arrived today with explicit instructions that it must be returned.

The Sumter Guards date back to 1819, which happens to be the year Alabama became a state, and along with the naval head gear, Boykin received a copy of the "History of the Sumter Guards" written in verse.

The whole thing was arranged by Rep. Mendel Rivers of Charleston, S.C., as a testimonial to Boykin's successful fight to abolition of the customs collector's districts at Mobile, Charleston and several other cities.

Shortly thereafter, in June 1959, at a powwow in Jacksonville, Florida, Frank spoke with clairvoyance and focused on two men, both of whom would, within five years, become president of the United States. What he said was:

> As a presidential possibility there is no finer statesman available right now than Texas' Lyndon Johnson, who has been led along for years by House Speaker Sam Rayburn. The Speaker, by the way, has been asked by many to enter the race, but each time he says he has too many things to do in the House. He is a Senator John Kennedy; he is also a capable man, like his great father; and religion should not be a handicap to him in any way. Remember, Alabama voted for Al Smith when he ran for President in 1928. People are more broadminded today. If anything, we need more religion in government, all religion.
>
> At this juncture fields of Democratic wishful are already getting ready. Senator John F. Kennedy of Massachusetts, with his eye on the White House, was eager and his bankrolled publicity were industrial, sounding the Kennedy trumpets via press, television and radio, paving the way for the costliest political campaign in presidential history. Senator Hubert Humphrey of Minnesota was making gestures though lacking money and the irresistible Kennedy charm. Senator Lyndon Johnson was involved in the chores of Senate Majority Leader to gear up for political race. He had no time for speech making or delegate hunting. If he had any White House aspirations at this moment, he kept them under wraps.

By midyear of 1959, a poll of fifty-six of the Democratic solons in the upper chamber had revealed their choice for the presidential nomination. Of these, seventeen favored Johnson; four stood up for Senator John F. Kennedy; Senator Hubert Humphrey, former Governor Mennen Williams of Michigan and Adlai Stevenson each had two; and Senator Albert Gore and Governor Robert Meyner of New Jersey brought up the rear with one each.

The poll did not reflect the sentiment of the nation, but it revealed what most of the Senate membership thought about the potential candidates. It indicated that Johnson's leadership of the Senate was so constructive he could well be expected to exhibit the same brand of mastery if elevated to the nation's top executive office.

The Boykins had mingled with the Johnsons freely. But Frank also had the same relationship with Senator John Kennedy, whom he had known since he and JFK's father, Joseph Kennedy, were acquaintances engaged in joint business ventures. Frank felt either would make a good candidate.

Political deals were being aired. A suggestion of a Johnson-Kennedy ticket was buzzed about but the Kennedy camp was demanding all or nothing.

In September 1959, there was a bitter battle over the Landrum-Griffin bill that was barreled through the House. The measure was designed to curb labor abuses that the American people had wished to see corrected. Frank was so persuasive with his undercover maneuvering that columnist Drew Pearson named him as one of the nineteen key personalities in the Dixie Democrat-Republican coalition who was able to block, defeat or pass legislation at will.

Landrum-Griffin was a reform measure needed to check the growing menace and misdeeds of labor racketeers. It was the first major overhaul of the nation's labor laws since the Taft Hartley Act of 1947. The bill was a substitute for the Kennedy-Ervin bill, which lacked a lot of meaning. The Union bosses opposed it with open threats of reprisals at the polls. Backbones stiffened and the legislators switched to a bill that would answer the demands of the American people, including thousands of labor's rank and file.

The key fight raged over substituting the Landrum-Griffin Bill for the wishy-washy bill for which Senator John F. Kennedy was the chief spokesman. It was a bill branded as "vengeful legislation."

On the crucial vote to discard the Kennedy-Erwin Bill and substitute the Landrum-Griffin Bill, one hundred and ninety-four Republicans and ninety-four Democrats, mostly Southerners, massed behind the latter and got it through. The next day, by a vote of 229 to 201, the House approved the Landrum bill. It was a defeat for organized labor and a crushing victory for President Eisenhower.

* * *

The year of the election, Frank was given a huge honor in his home state:

> *City Commission, Frank Boykin Shrine Day*
> *City of Mobile, November 5, 1960*
> *State of Alabama, Mayor's Proclamation*
>
> WHEREAS, the Nobles of Abba Temple and the Ancient Order of Nobles of the Mystic Shrine have constantly engaged in benevolent enterprises that have done much to alleviate pain and suffering among our citizenry, and
>
> WHEREAS their work in caring for the crippled children in our community, without regard to their religion, or race, has gained for them our respect and gratitude, and
>
> WHEREAS, the Honorable Frank Boykin, Congressman from this Congressional District, has done so much for so many people irrespective of their position in life and has been a great credit to the Shrine and all in works, and
>
> WHEREAS, his two sons, Bob and Jack, are being initiated in the Fall Ceremonial Class November 5, 1960, and the Nobles of Abba Temple saw fit to name the class "The Frank Boykin Class," in honor of the Congressman.
>
> NOW, THEREFORE, by the power vested in me as Mayor of the City of Mobile, I declare Saturday, November 5, 1960, Frank Boykin Shrine Day.
>
> Henry R. Luscher, Sr. Mayor
City of Mobile, Alabama

In early May 1960, the voters of Alabama's First District had given Frank another honor: an overwhelming endorsement for a fourteenth term in the House. They believed him when he said that twenty-five years' seniority in Congress was a precious asset not to be discarded lightly—that, in addition to his commitments and congressional know-how. Each re-election increased his power to render greater service to the people of Southern Alabama, which was his life's work. And, luckily, he possessed the drive of a locomotive.

At the time, racial issues were alarming the entire South. The federal government, abetted by vote-hungry Northern politicians, was determined, openly, to incite the black segment of the South to acts of violence against white institutions. Black factions occurred throughout Southern municipalities. The "solid South" was splintering.

The 1960 Democratic National Convention proved that the U.S. dollar earned its traditional place in politics. In Los Angeles, the Kennedy millions behind JFK and the Democratic Party were like a solid-gold Rock of Gibraltar to stand in (similar to what would happen in the elections of 2008).

It was no surprise when Lyndon Johnson was announced as the Democratic nominee for vice president in July 1960, and Frank made it clear he would support the Kennedy-Johnson ticket.

Senator John Kennedy was the undisputed front-runner throughout the race. He was only forty-three, educated in public and private schools, received a BS in political science with honors at Harvard, and attended, for a short time, business school at Stanford University. During World War II, as a Navy lieutenant, Kennedy was known for commanding a PT boat. He worked as an INS correspondent, covering the UN conference in San Francisco, the Potsdam Conference, and the 1945 British elections.

His father was known for his principal business interests of banking, shipbuilding, and movie theater chains, as well as serving in government-appointed posts, including as ambassador to England. John married Jacqueline, who was educated at Vassar, the Sorbonne, and George Washington University; she was also multilingual.

The Massachusetts Catholic senator favored separation of Church and State. He served on the House Education and Labor Committee and on the Labor and Public Welfare Committee in the Senate. In the Upper House, he was a member of the Government Operations Committee, the Select Committee on Small Business, the McClellan Investigating Committee, the Joint Economic Committee, and the Foreign Relations Committee. He voted with most of his party 70 percent of the time and consistently voted against conservative coalition proposals of Republican and Southern Democrats.

Kennedy favored preservation of the family farm, encouragement of co-ops and assurance that farmers would get a fair share of the nation's income. He also favored an increased soil conservation reserve. He was very pro-civil rights and for enforcement powers for attorney general (a position that would later be filled by his brother Robert). He had a firm belief in policies for all federal agencies, federal anti-bomb legislation with enforcement by the FBI and right-to-vote protection by federal referees. He was strongly pro-labor and on the liberal side of his party.

Frank urged his constituents to follow his lead. "The Deep South," he said, "will be wise to support the Democratic Party. Give us a Democratic president so we can get our rivers developed and this will become one of the greatest and fastest growing industrial areas in the world."

Alabama was becoming a house divided as the Republicans incited scores of old-line, staunch Democrats to desert the party to support the Nixon-Lodge bandwagon. Topflight commentators and newspaper editors were deluging the state with warnings of tragedy in the South if the Kennedy-Johnson team won in November.

On October 8, 1960, Frank received a surprising letter from his friend Harry Truman, who cold-shouldered the Kennedy candidacy shortly after the Los Angeles convention. In this letter, Truman recanted his earlier distaste for the outsider of the Democratic ticket:

> *Dear Frank,*
>
> *Now, as never before, it seems to me, there is a need for us to submerge whatever differences may exist among us within our own Party and fight for a Democratic victory.*
>
> *I simply do not believe the United States can stand four more years of another Republican President in the White House. We have lost ground in the past 8 years under a Republican President. Another Republican administration and a Republican President could only be expected to produce continued stagnation and a backward policy to continue an 1896 program, and this is 1960. With Nixon in the White House, there will be a complete breakdown in the domestic and foreign affairs of our government. I wonder if you want another 1929.*
>
> *As you know, John Kennedy was not my first choice for the nomination. However, he is a very able young man, and, in my opinion, a man of integrity and honor. These qualities I*

regard as essential in a President of the United States. Also, it is very important to remember that in choosing a President we not only select the man who occupies that office, but we also determine the Party in control of the Executive Branch of our Government. History proves it is better for the Nation and the people when the Democrats are in control of the White House and the Congress.

It seems to me our choice is clear. We know how important it is to have State and Congressional candidates who will support the national ticket. The better the national ticket runs, the more it helps State and Congressional candidates.

From my viewpoint, there is much to be gained and nothing to be lost by working together and doing our best for the whole ticket. I shall be campaigning just as I have done in times past, not because I want anything for myself, but because the country needs a leader in the White House and leaders in Congress. I ask you to join in all out support for the Democratic ticket.

Sincerely Yours,
Harry S. Truman

On October 11, 1960, Frank sent the following reply:

Honorable Harry S. Truman
Independence, Missouri

My dear Harry:
Thanks for your good letter. Of course, I am doing everything I can for the Democratic ticket. We would have no trouble at all, if either you, Sam Rayburn or Lyndon Johnson headed the ticket. You and I have worked with and served with every one of the four candidates, and we will carry on, whatever happens, but it would be better, so much better, if we had a Democratic President and Vice President. Of course, I was for Lyndon Johnson all the way, but I am for Jack Kennedy and Lyndon Johnson all the way and am working day and night.

I am enclosing you a story about our meeting. We had our Speaker Rayburn here with us; also, Lister Hill, Governor Patterson, George Grant and many other notables, and what a wonderful time we had; but there is no trouble except this religious question, and it is serious—very, very serious, and I think it is the only question we have to answer.

I wish you could have heard Sam Rayburn's speech. I had a record made of it and could send it out there, or wherever you think we might need it. Of course, you know Senator Lister Hill is always wonderful, and he is the one that brought out that Nixon had voted against Social Security, T.V.A., free school lunches, vocational education, vocational rehabilitation and so many other things. I had forgotten about it. However, I think Kennedy is handling himself well. I think Nixon showed up very much better in this last debate they had than he did in the first, but I think Jack was better, even in that one. Sam Rayburn and a group of us were at our hunting lodge at McIntosh, Alabama, and heard it from there, without a big crowd around us—just our families.

How I wish you and Mrs. Truman would come down sometime. We really have a pretty good place there. We have over 100,000 acres there, 400 miles of roads and 30 miles of lake, 1,000 miles of fence and lots of the best colored people in the world that have been there since they've been born.

What I think you should concentrate on is this Attorney General Rogers, who is causing so much trouble; also, the so-called Dr. or Reverend Luther King that caused so much trouble in the Capitol of Montgomery, where Jeff Davis was sworn in as head of the Confederacy. Of course, you will remember that Dick Nixon did say that this half breed Dr. Luther King, who is causing trouble in Washington, and you will remember when he visited the White House, that Nixon did say he was one of the greatest men that ever lived and many, many other things. I think I wrote you a very long letter about this; I don't know.

Anyway, we had quite a storm here the other day when we had a show for Sam Rayburn, Lister Hill, the Governor and all of the other prominent people we had. We had practically every state official here, and you will note from a letter, if you have time to read this letter, which is too damn long, to a great friend and hunting partner of mine that owns the Montgomery Advertiser and the Alabama Journal. He made every nickel he has out of the Democrats. Every elected officer in the State of Alabama is a Democrat, and we had them all sign up the other night. You might use a few of the things we have in this letter. It is awfully hard to get on a friend like I have had to get on Furman Hudson. Furman Hudson is about your age and my age and should know better. Of course, we like what Senator Goldwater said, but if the Republicans liked it so much, why didn't they pick him as their President or Vice-President? What he said about the Supreme Court not being the law of the land, and that the Constitution was, you and I have known this all the time. Our Chief Justice, Ed Livingston, made that speech in New York two years ago. Lister Hill has been preaching it ever since we had the decision.

I remember the fine and wonderful things that Walter George, Dick Russell, Harry Byrd and all the people had to say about Lyndon Johnson. I also remember—and you and I came to the Capitol at the same time—that Lyndon Johnson, when he did come a little later as secretary, I think to Dick Kleeberg, was only making $125.00 a month. Now, think what he is doing—leading the greatest body on earth. Well, I don't know—you can find an excuse for most anything you want to, but you and I know Lyndon Johnson is a brilliant man, a great statesman, a great legislator and has done one of the most outstanding jobs that's ever been done since George Washington himself was President of these United States.

I have covered a few of these things in my letter to Furman Hudson, the owner of these papers in Montgomery, Alabama and I have covered some of the things that Sam Rayburn said; and by the way, our Governor, John Patterson, down here is doing a superhuman job. We were out all-day Sunday. We will be meeting Lyndon Johnson on his special train Thursday. I am leaving nothing undone that I know how to do. I am having a luncheon today for a great group, and we are meeting everyday and every night, but we have trouble here; there is no doubt about it. Our Baptist preacher said Sunday, so I am told by one of my associates, that if we elected a Catholic as President of the United States, the Protestant religion would be swept from the face of the earth. Of course, they don't know that we have a Senate and House that makes these laws. The President either signs them or vetoes them, and that if we are right enough, we can override the vetoes. That ought to be gotten over.

Another that should gotten over, and I covered this in my letter to you some time ago about Dick Nixon, is Little Rock. That was the most terrible that has ever happened in the history, and Dick Nixon told me it was terrible, it was murder; it was destruction talking about the States Rights. Well, you saw what the people of Arkansas did; they gave Faubus a four to one majority in the State of Arkansas, and I think he beat four opponents all at one time.

Another point, I think, and a good point is, that when you left the White House, you left the communists ten thousand miles away in Korea. Now they have kept on coming on until they are just eight minutes from Key West, where you have spent much of your time, and you know about all about that, and they are only an hour by jet from where I am sitting right now, before daybreak, writing you this letter on the Dictaphone.

I know Jack Kennedy; I know his father. He used to be Chairman of the Maritime Commission and would come before our Merchant Marine & Fisheries Committee every week, and sometimes two and three times. He is a good businessman; he is a god American. Jack Kennedy comes to the House on crutches, where he had been wounded in the war. He did a good job there, and I think he really is very, very smart—smarter than I thought he was. I think he has made a wonderful impression and is working hard and has brains, ability and energy, and Lord knows, I am very close to Lyndon Johnson and Sam Rayburn. You will remember the famous dinner we gave him.

Well, we are going to give him another one when this is over and get everybody back together—win, lose or draw, because we've got to get closer together; but if you, Harry Truman, were there in the White House, I believe you would kick this big bully Khrushchev out. You don't invite that kind of people into your house or your office or your home; and Lord knows that communist Castro—we are going to sit still here and let him ruin that beautiful country.

I imagine I put in the letter, I don't know, that I am sending you a copy of, that we have just had an inquiry last week from Cuba, that if we could furnish three million gallons of fresh water a day, because we are expecting Castro and his communists to poison our water there in our Naval Base in Cuba or to blow up the water works, they would like to have it. Isn't that a hell of a thing?

Well, we only have a few more days left. In just twenty-some-odd days from now we will know who God and the people want to be President and Vice-President, and whoever He wants, we will certainly take them and get in there and work and work hard.

Thanks for writing me, Harry. Write every single one of your old friends. You have the list there but get it out to them quick and get it out to them by Air Mail. Sam Rayburn is doing a superhuman job. That old boy still speaks without notes, still doesn't have to wear glasses and God has his hand on his shoulder, and regardless of what happens on November 8, Sam Rayburn will be Speaker and Lyndon Johnson will have charge in the Senate, and regardless of who is President and Vice-President of the United States, we will be able to control the situation, and I know this proposition has put us closer and closer together. And we must do that more than ever before because it looks like the whole world is against us and wants to take everything on earth we have. I love Mexico and have been doing business there for over forty years, and one of my friends from England wrote me the other day that the Russians had 6,000 communists in their embassy in Mexico. I have a great friend down there that represents us, of Basham Finge & Corren. Cordell Mull sent us to them forty years ago, and Antonio Corren is our lawyer. I have written him fully about this. We also have a great Ambassador there, the Honorable Robert Hill, and I am writing Bob Hill, too. Of course, Bob Hill would know about this. I wrote him the day I received this letter. I haven't heard from him yet, but it is time for all of us to do our dead level best, and I know you are doing that and I know we are doing that. Our entire Alabama Delegation are fighting with all our might to try to keep some little part of States' Rights and some little part of our way of life.

Ocllo and my entire family join me in love to you, Mrs. Truman, Margaret, her husband and the children.

God Bless and keep you and give you strength to keep on keeping on is the wish of your old friend.

God Bless you again,

Sincerely your old friend,
Frank W. Boykin
Member of Congress

On October 14, vice presidential candidate Lyndon Johnson's 'Campaign Special' rolled into Alabama on the final lap of a five-day whistle-stop promenade through eight Southern states. In Pensacola, the Johnson caravan's last stop in Florida, Frank shepherded a large delegation of political leaders aboard Johnson's private car, where Governor Patterson formally welcomed the Texan to Alabama. From Pensacola, the Alabamians rode with the candidate to various points along his route.

Accompanying Frank was his wife, Ocllo, veteran of at least ten of her husband's re-election campaigns. While Alabama's notables were recharging their campaign batteries by having contact with the candidate, Frank gave Johnson a fast run-down of the powerhouse performance he and his campaign allies were staging to put the Democratic ticket over in South Alabama.

"If we can carry South Alabama, we can win the state," he told Johnson confidently. "And I believe we will."

Lady Bird Johnson played her part in stride. An old hand at campaigning, she never missed a cue, which at this point was to talk about her Alabama kinfolk and background. Attired in a chic red dress, she appeared on the rear platform with her husband and teenage daughter, Lucy Baines. It was a gala stopover. Admirers and greeters swarmed about her, inundating them with flowers, hams, jars of Southern sweets and other homemade delicacies.

Ocllo and Lady Bird were long-time fellow-riders on the Washington merry-go-round. After the train left Pensacola, the two ladies retired to a quiet spot for a tete-a-tete. That morning before leaving Mobile, Ocllo had put into her handbag a humble but age-old symbol of luck she often carried, a rabbit's foot.

"I brought you something," said Ocllo, reaching into her handbag.

"A rabbit's foot!" exclaimed Lady Bird, her dark eyes lighting up when she saw it.

"I brought it especially for you," assured Ocllo.

"Just what we need...how nice!"

"But it isn't the left foot of a graveyard rabbit. Just a plain plantation rabbit's that's brought me lots of luck. I won a thirty-six-thousand-dollar house with a dollar raffle ticket. Frank bought twenty tickets. He gave the girls in his office each a ticket and one to each of the men in our family. Anyway, mine was the lucky one and I can't help feeling that the rabbit's foot did it. We gave the house to the Baptist College in Mobile and Frank gave me a pin to console me. Hold on to it and rub it now and then," suggested Ocllo. "I've carried this rabbit's foot on every one of Frank's campaigns. He was always a winner. It'll bring you luck."

One hundred miles from Pensacola, at Flomaton, Alabama, the Boykins left the train regretfully.

Lady Bird exhibited the rabbit's foot to Lyndon, who called out from the platform as the train pulled away, "Folks, we've won the election. Ocllo Boykin has given Lady Bird a rabbit's foot!"

Ten days later, the mailman brought Ocllo a letter written on LBJ Ranch letterhead and dated October 20, 1960. It said:

Dear Mrs. Boykin:

I am clutching that rabbit's foot for all it is worth and thank you so much. Nobody but you would have thought to bring me such a needed and valuable addition to our efforts.

Very best wishes to both the Boykins and deep appreciation for joining us on the train.

Sincerely,
Lady Bird

On election night, Frank and Ocllo, as well as millions of Americans, sat in their home listening to the election returns. The chips were being counted; the payoff was at hand. At midnight, before retiring, Frank called Western Union and dictated the following telegram:

Hon. John F. Kennedy
Hyannis port, Massachusetts

Well, we are doing our very best and hope when morning comes, we can address you as Mr. President instead of Senator. We have left nothing undone. God Bless you and yours,
Ocllo and Frank Boykin.

On November 13, the Associated Press totaled up the presidential popular votes cast in Alabama. It was the largest Republican vote in the history of the state up to then. Northern Alabama had given Richard Nixon a sizable majority, but Frank's South Alabama drive had swung the state's election to John Kennedy and Lyndon Johnson.

Looks like the rabbit's foot paid off!

But the election left Alabama facing one of the most complex, controversial problems in her history, a political Pandora's box. The Census Bureau in Washington had promptly released the grim news that as a result of the 1960 Census, Alabama must redraw her congressional districts and reduce her representation in the House from nine to eight members. Reshuffling Alabama's counties into one less district was a task that required the patience of Job.

Mid-December brought Frank a letter from an old friend and fellow worker in the money-making business, Joseph P. Kennedy, father of the president elect. Written on letterhead bearing the superscription "JOSEPH P. KENNEDY, HYANNISPORT, MASSACHUSETTS," it ran:

> *Dear Frank:*
>
> *I want to tell you: you are the champion letter writer of all times. I think we ought to have you in Europe, South America, Asia, and Africa; and, if we did, I am very sure we would get more information about these countries that we could get out of the whole State Department.*
>
> *Anyway, you know I am very grateful for your goodwill, good wishes and your help. I hope I will be seeing you at the time of the Inauguration. With my warmest personal regards,*
> *Sincerely, Joe*

On January 13, 1961, the scene shifted to the winter home of Joseph P. Kennedy at Palm Beach, where the president-elect was enjoying some relaxation before assuming the duties of the presidency. Frank and Ocllo were the guests of Florida's automobile tycoon C.J. Johnson at his home in Palm Beach. In the Johnson party was also Congressman Mendel Rivers, chairman of the Armed Forces Committee of the House and his wife, and Secretary of Commerce Luther Hodges.

On returning from a fishing party on the Johnson yacht at dark, on January 12, they found a young man sitting on the porch in slacks and sweatshirt, but with no hat. It was President-Elect John Kennedy. He had waited about an hour. After pleasantries, Kennedy said, "Frank, I want you to bring this group down to lunch tomorrow. My father and mother will be with us." He then hopped in his car and sped away.

Frank assumed at once that Kennedy wanted to pressure him on the Rules Committee vote. The next day, on arriving at the Kennedy domicile, the Boykins were welcomed warmly like old, esteemed friends. Waiting to greet the party were "Old Joe" and his wife, Rose, Vice President-Elect Lyndon Johnson and a scattering of the Kennedy entourage. The president-elect was swimming but came up shortly, greeted the visitors and vanished into the house only to reappear handsome and bubbling with wit. The lunch was served on the front lawn, with John at the head of the table. He promptly announced, "I don't know what the protocol is going to be, but I want Ocllo to sit on my right and Frank on my left." He then seated his other guests. He asked his mother, Rose, to sit on Frank's left, with "Old Joe" next to her while the rest of the party arranged themselves.

John Kennedy had often teased Frank about his "love" platform. As the guests took their seats, Kennedy explained, "Frank and I have lots of things to catch up on." He got to the point: "Frank, do you think Old Joe would make a good United States senator?"

Frank enthusiastically answered, "You couldn't do better. As you know, I have known Joe, Rose and their family for twenty-five years. Joe and I saw a great deal of each other during World War II when he was chief of the Maritime Commission, and I was a member of the Merchant Marine and Fisheries Committee of the House. He has brains, ability, energy and worlds of experience."

Kennedy pursued the idea of senator for Joe Kennedy no further, but apparently his father overheard Frank's reply and beamed, "If I had one more friend like Frank Boykin, I wouldn't need any more friends."

John Kennedy got more confidential. He dropped his voice. "Frank, first, I want you to know how much I appreciate all you did to swing Alabama my way in the election. Sam Rayburn and Lyndon Johnson, both told me about it. Now, Frank, what can I do for you?" asked Kennedy pointedly.

"Very little, but since you asked it, there are two things I want. I'd appreciate your appointing General W.K. Wilson, Jr. as chief of Army engineers. And I have a dear friend, Homer Guenther, brother of General Alfred Gruenther, who is an assistant to President Eisenhower. I'd appreciate your keeping him on the job at the White House."

"Is that all I can do for you?" asked Kennedy.

"That's all you can do for me and I think that it is enough."

"It shall be done," assured Kennedy, who made a short memorandum of it on the spot.

John Kennedy chatted quietly as the luncheon progressed, but not a word about the Rules Committee issue came up from the moment Frank arrived until he left.

Shortly before the party broke up, Joe Kennedy took Frank aside and asked him to write a letter to him and his wife, Rose, recommending their son, Robert Kennedy, for the attorney general's appointment in his brother's Cabinet. Frank airmailed the letter the next day from Washington, highly endorsing him with his credentials for the Cabinet post.

Later, Frank said, "I believe Jack was planning to make his father, Joseph Kennedy, United States senator from Massachusetts. John Kennedy did not say that in so many words, but his question indicated such a move was being considered. They would have easily done it and probably would have; had not Joe been stricken ill."

Back in Washington Frank wrote a letter to Rayburn repeating what he had already been warning:

> *I cannot go along with you on packing the Rules Committee. If the Rules Committee is packed, it will ruin many of your lifetime friends in Texas, Alabama, and all over the South. Now I wish people would tell you the truth and what they are telling everyone else. Please, for God's sake, Sam, and for the sake of this nation and for all mankind, try to do something to keep this fight from coming up on the floor where anything can happen.*

He also telegraphed President Kennedy, urging him to stay clear of the *"fight between our two great Congressmen, Speaker Sam Rayburn and Representative Howard Smith. In my judgment, if this fight continues, it will destroy my beloved friend, Sam, just as it did Speaker Cannon when he was Speaker so many years ago."*

On January 31, 1961, Sam Rayburn won the fight in the House by a cliffhanger, with a margin of four votes. It was such a narrow margin that it left many friendships broken.

Frank had said, "All sorts of things were promised in the fight to pack the Rules Committee. They even offered me a place on the Committee, but I wouldn't have it for the world. Had the rest of the Alabama delegation kept their promises to me, we would have defeated Rayburn."

The estrangement between Frank and Sam Rayburn over the Rules Committee decision was unresolved. But unknown then was that Rayburn had less than a year to live.

CHAPTER NINETEEN

JFK's Speech to the Gridiron Club

In 1961, Frank Boykin came up with the idea of producing a Congressional anthology that would bear the title *Fifty Years of the Best Stories in Congress*. During his almost three decades in the House, he had filed away in his campaign arsenal good, publishable stories and anecdotes. He saw the cloakroom, committee meetings and other gatherings of his colleagues as having the potential for good stories that infiltrated the actual lawmaking.

Congress abounded in wit, with the legislators telling good tales with which to appeal to the voters. Enclosing the best stories in a book for the nation seemed like a great idea.

Frank dispatched a round robin to every member of the House and Senate, appealing for contributions. Included in his solicitation were former United States senator and president of the U.S., John F. Kennedy. Frank knew the Kennedy wit and figured he'd have great stories to contribute to the book. A note from Postmaster General Lawrence F. O'Brien said, *"The President hopes to come up with something worthy of the title and, if he meets with success, we shall send it along."* The President meant business, for a fortnight later, Frank received a letter from the White House saying, *"The President is making available to you the enclosed copy of his speech at the Gridiron Club Dinner on March 15, 1958, and you are free to use it in any way you like."*

The speech had presumably never been published. It gives insight into the wit, heart, and mind of John F. Kennedy. When the president gave this speech, he adhered to the rules: no president is allowed to talk longer than five minutes. Two other rules distinguish the club's set of laws: (1) ladies are always present; in other words, no off-color stories are permitted, and (2) reporters as such are never present, meaning the president's speech is never reported.

Published in the book *Everything's Made for Love* (by Edward Boykin, page 193) is the following:

"Gridiron is the Club of the newspaper fraternity in Washington. The name is suggestive of the agonies to which distinguished guests are subjected to the Club's fun makers. The President is usually given a thorough going over while the politicos are roasted on the Club's merry gridiron. President Cleveland, who found no humor in the idea, turned down the invitation of the Club that was founded in 1885.

"President Kennedy's typewritten speech bears this injunction: 'This speech is not for publication, quotation or other reproduction in whole or in part. It is reprinted here only for private distribution to personal friends who have requested a copy.'

"However, President Kennedy unlocked it for Frank W. Boykin to use 'in any way you like.'"

The text of the speech is as follows:

> *Mr. McKelway, Mr. Vice President, Mr. Chief Justice, Gentlemen of the Gridiron:*
>
> *I have just received the following wire from my generous daddy: "Dear Jack, Don't buy a single vote more than necessary—I'll be damned if I'm going to pay for a landslide."*
>
> *I am grateful to my father for his support—but I am even more grateful to Mr. Sam Rayburn. At the last Democratic Convention, if he had not recognized the Tennessee and Oklahoma delegations when he did, I might have won that race with Senator Kefauver—and my political career would now be over.*
>
> *I have been told tonight that if I will only not reveal the truth about the members of the Gridiron Club in front of their houses, they in turn can insure me the Democratic Presidential nomination. I am not the first politician to be thus tempted by the newspaper fraternity. When Speaker Joe Cannon half a*

century ago told the ANPA that, in exchange for his opposition to the newsprint tariff, the publishers would deliver him the Presidency, Speaker Cannon removed his cigar and replied: "You know, 2000 years ago or so, another fellow was tempted like this. And the tempter led him up on the highest mountain top; and showed him all the kingdoms of the world, and all the valleys of milk and honey—and he said, 'If you will fall and worship me, all of this will I give you.' But the truth of the matter is," Speaker Cannon went on, "he didn't own one damn inch of it."

I am not sure that the members of the Gridiron club do either.

"Frankly, I am not now making any plans for the Presidency. Should I be elected, I do hope that Bishop Bromley Oxnam of the P.A.D.U. will be my personal envoy to the Vatican—and he's instructed to open negotiations for that Trans-Atlantic Tunnel immediately.

Otherwise, I am not campaigning. It is true that I have traveled—some because I told Paul Butler that I would be willing to go to all states with promising Democratic candidates. I should have known that we have no other kind.

I make these statements in confidence. But are they safe? I understand, for instance, that the Gridiron Club files have recently been broken into. Someone stole your officer's election returns for the next six years.

Moreover, I have been told that this is a predominantly Republican organization—and that your affairs usually open with the prayer that Divine Providence will remain under the protection of the Administration.

But I am here bearing an olive branch—to unveil a new Democratic strategy. If we can't lick the press, we'll join them. So, I say, Newspapermen and Democrats, let us unite!

Under our regime, all reporters can go to Communist China without official protection—in fact I'm drawing up now a list of those I want to see go first. Under our regime, you can stand as close as you want to the missile launchings at Cape Canaveral, we'll report to the press all confidential high-level conferences, such as this recent conversation between the President and the Secretary of State, revealed here for the first time: "Where did you go" "Out!" "What did you do?" "Nothing!"

Now you can help us in a few ways, too. The first is to screen all our potential candidates for 1960.

I dreamed about 1960 myself the other night, and I told Stuart Symington and Lyndon Johnson about it in the Cloakroom yesterday. I told them how the Lord came into my bedroom, anointed my head, and said: "John Kennedy, I hereby appoint you President of the United States." Stu Symington said: "That's strange, Jack, because I, too, had a similar dream last night, in which the Lord anointed me and declared me, Stuart Symington, President of the United States and outer space." And Lyndon Johnson said: "That's very interesting, gentlemen, because I, too, had a similar dream last night—and I don't remember anointing either one of you!"

We do have lots of candidates. A recent A.P. survey asked each Senator about his preference for the Presidency—and 96 Senators each received a vote.

One possible ticket would be Sonny Williams and Orval Faubus—that way the voters would hear a real debate of the issues without ever tuning in the Republicans.

I do not deny that the Democrats have their differences. The Democratic Advisory Council has succeeded in splitting our Party right down the middle—and that gives us more unity than we've had in 20 years.

But we want you to help by reporting all Republicans feuds in full. Some of them are diminishing, I must admit. Vice President Nixon and Sherman Adams, for example, decided to bury the hatchet—in Harold Stassen. Mr. Stassen announces he will run for Governor of Pennsylvania. He has already been Governor of Minnesota and that leaves only 46 states still in jeopardy.

I do not say that Sherman Adams alone is responsible for these key decisions. All I say is that the Constitution will prohibit him from seeking a third term.

But the key Republican, of course, is my old friend Dick Nixon, the most popular man in his Party. Some people used to say that Dick was doing the basement work over at Republican Headquarters. But now they've given those janitorial duties to Sherman Adams, and moved Dick upstairs to teach the men's Bible class.

But now we turn to an area where we can really join forces usefully—getting the facts on the recession.

As I interpret the President, we're now at the end of the beginning of the upturn of the downturn. Every bright spot the White House finds in the economy is like the policeman bending over the body in the alley, who says cheerfully: "Two of his wounds are fatal—but the other one's not so bad."

No anti-recession program for the farmers has been announced except Mr. Benson's hope to get the Government out of the farming business. The farmer's program is to get Mr. Benson out of the governing business.

Amazing as it may seem, the Republicans have learned to increase the cost of living in a recession—a real feat. If they get it up much higher, they can put a dog in it.

But whatever our failings as Republicans and Democrats—they are many—the fact remains that we together are the only instruments of popular government that the American people possess. We are all they have.

The question is whether a Democratic society—with its freedom of choice, its breadth of opportunity, with its range of alternatives—can meet the single-minded advance of the Communists.

Our decisions are more subtle than dramatic. Our far-flung interests are more complex than consistent—our crises are more chronic than easily solved.

Can a nation have organized and governed such as ours endure that is the real question. Have we the nerve and the will?

Have we got what it takes to carry through in an age whereas never before our very survival is at stake, where we and the Russians have the power to destroy one-quarter of the earth's population—a feat not accomplished since Cain and Able? Can we carry through in an age where we will witness not only new break-throughs in weapons of destruction but also a race for the mastery of the sky and the rain, the ocean and the tides, the inside of the earth and the inside of men's minds?

We are moving ahead along a knife-edged path which requires leadership better equipped than any since Lincoln's day to make clear to our people the vast spectrum of our challenges.

In the words of Woodrow Wilson: "We must neither run with the crowd nor deride it but seek sober counsel for it—and for ourselves."

CHAPTER TWENTY

Gerrymandering

Gerrymandering Alabama's thirty-year-old county district layout was full of pitfalls. The vital question to be resolved was: which of the nine incumbents would be lost? It was obvious no one would willingly lay his neck on the block. The first law of politics is self-preservation.

Remapping the state's political geography involved everybody associated with the present district alignments: congressmen, probate judges, county commissioners and almost every other public officer at every level of government. It made a massive melee of personal feuds, gut-fighting and angry shrieks in the state's politics.

In September 1961, after much debate, the state legislators adopted the so-called "nine to eight" plan that would pass along to the voters the solution of the problem of re-districting the state. The procedure was three-phased: first the nine incumbents and other qualified candidates must compete in a statewide sweepstakes in their respective districts, as presently set up. Second, the winners of these nine contests must then engage in a run-off state primary contest. Third, the top eight of the nine district nominees would then be declared the Democratic nominees in the November general elections in a Democratic-ruled state in the South.

By December 1961, for many months the newspaper headlines were full of the collapse of several Maryland saving and loan associations. A federal grand jury was delving into the defunct institutions with a fine-tooth comb. The key figure was J. Kenneth Edlin, a sixty-three-year-old entrepreneur, who was charged for attempted mail fraud.

Frank had been associated with Edlin in a Maryland land development and was unaware that Edlin had a record of a previous conviction in federal court. He had interceded with Attorney General Robert Kennedy on behalf of Edlin, who was to be sentenced on his latest conviction on January 19, 1962. The press got wind of this and started an assassination attempt on Frank.

The news from Washington to the local papers was a headline: "RICH BOYKIN GETTING RICHER, CASE REVEALS." A leading Birmingham paper broke it to its readers. The story became a vote killer and was spread throughout every town and village in Alabama, wherever anyone would be casting a vote in the nine-to-eight battles.

The Boykin-Edlin association was headlines for weeks. In a sensational "revelation" on May 6, 1961, the day after America's pioneer astronaut, Commander Alan B. Shepherd, Jr., soared into space, Frank offered the nation's hero a new twenty-five-thousand-dollar house, with a swimming pool and all the amenities, in a new development nearby Waldorf, Maryland, where Frank owned over eight thousand acres. Shepherd's presence would give wonderful publicity to the enterprise that Frank described as "a Heaven on Earth." To make matters worse, Frank had asked President Kennedy to make the presentation. Even though it was not the first time a promoter had sought presidential blessing for his product, which, in this matter, was a housing project, lots and new homes, the press was like a flock of mockingbirds seeking any news of this matter.

Later, there was a flood of manufacturers asking Commander Shepherd to promote their products. Among other recipients of homes donated by admirers were General Grant, Daniel Webster, General Douglas MacArthur and many others.

On February 2, 1962, when Frank turned seventy-seven, he was at a historic luncheon in the Old Senate Chamber in the Capitol, where he was hailed by colleagues, friends, and President Kennedy. The president had not taken seriously the newspaper insinuations against Frank. It appeared to be a vendetta against him by the Justice Department and the press.

Frank had twenty-seven years seniority, with only ten members that stood between him and the top of the seniority ladder. He was the number-two Democrat on the Merchant Marine and Fisheries Committee, chairman of its Wildlife Sub-Committee and next in line for chairmanship of the full committee. He was also the fourth-ranking member of the Veterans Affair Committee. Surrounding Frank was prosperity, love and glory that few grasps.

Bob Boykin said, "I recall writing with my brothers and sisters a telegram we sent to 'Dear Mendel Rivers': 'Will you please read this hastily written poem at Papa's birthday party?'"

The telegram was received on February 21, 1962, at Mendel' office:

> TO PAPA:
> IN FOURTEEN HUNDRED AND NINETY-TWO
> COLUMBUS SAILED THE OCEAN BLUE
> AND FOUND THE SHORES FOR US AND YOU:
> SOMEHOW, WE FEEL THAT EVEN THEN
> WHEN HOPE WAS WEARING PRETTY THIN:
> TO TEST FOR LIFE ON THE LAND HE SAW:
> HE SENT AHEAD A TURTLE DOVE
> AND HEARD THERE WITH A BRAND-NEW LAW
> THAT EVERYTHING'S MADE FOR LOVE
>
> IF CLEOPATRA, QUEEN OF THE NILE,
> NEEDED A NEW GENERAL WITH WHICH TO BEGUILE
> SHE WOULD HAVE SENT JULIUS AND MARK TO THE PLANK
> AND SENT IMMEDIATELY FOR A MAN NAMED FRANK:
>
> THIS IDLE CHATTER IS SIMPLY TO SAY:
> THAT YOU'D BE TOPS IN ANY DAY:
> WE HAVE THE IDEA THAT WHEN IT'S TIME
> FOR YOU TO JOIN OUR PAUL REVERE,
> ST. PETER WILL MEET YOU AND SAY, "STAY HERE"
> YOUR HEART IS SO BIG AND SO FORGIVING:
> SO WE HOPE YOU'RE LIKE MOSES
> AND YOUR LIFE WILL CLIMB AS THE MORNING ROSES
> OVER THE WALL INTO FOREVER,
> WITH YOUR WONDERFUL SMILE AND YOUR HELPING ENDEAVOR.

*AND TO YOUR NICE FRIENDS WHO HAVE GATHERED HERE
TO PAY TRIBUTE TO OUR DAD, WHO IS SO DEAR,
WE'D LIKE TO SAY THANK YOU TO EACH AND ALL
FOR COMING TODAY TO FILL THIS HALL.
YOU'RE THE FRIENDS OF WHICH HE HAS GREAT PRIDE
BECAUSE AMONG YOU THERE'S NO DIVIDE.
YOU MAY BE A DEMOCRAT OR A GOP
BUT IF YOU'RE HIS FRIEND, IT'S A TEE.
WE LOVE YOU DAD, THE VERY BEST IN THE LAND
BUT DON'T FORGET IT'S MOTHER WHO MADE YOU
SO GRAND.
HAPPY BIRTHDAY,*

                     THE BOYKIN CHILDREN

Hearing of Frank's seventy-seventh birthday party, the editor of *Decatur Daily* in Alabama wrote:

BOYKIN FOREVER YOUNG

> *Hilarious books could be written about Alabama's Frank Boykin, member of Congress from the Mobile District who turned 77 this week and with 27 years to his credit in Congress. Boykin is a wealthy man. He couldn't possibly know his own worth and neither could he estimate the cost of entertaining friends in Washington or Mobile or at his fabulous hunting preserve near McIntosh, Alabama. Who will you find there? Anybody, corporation presidents and Vice Presidents of the U.S. nation. Don't put it past Frank that JFK won't show up at the hunting grounds one of these days. Boykin is forever young, forever exuberant, and he tells his friends, 'If you can go to Heaven, come to Mobile.' He is a legend in his own right.*

Some newsman captured Frank and asked the congressman, "What do you think of this nine-to-eight plan?"

Frank spoke up confidently and suggested that the nine candidates pool their vote-getting activities by hiring a motorcade of buses large enough to tour the state and carry each congressman and his staff and his campaign literature, as well as a band to heat things up.

Frank said:

> *I spend my time between sessions of this Congress running around talking all over the State. I've been a congressman fourteen terms and they are mighty kind to me in my District and I glory in friends all over the State of Alabama, but now, this chasing all over the State by nine men seeking eight offices is likely to be mighty expensive. So, I arrived at a plan that has possibilities. Under my plan all nine of us, that is, all nine incumbents, would hire buses together, take along a band and tour the State where there are 67 counties. Each man would have 5 minutes to talk at every stop. They may get tired of hearing my 'Everything's Made for Love' but we'd get along just fine.*

Tireless, seemingly ageless, Frank announced his re-election the moment the state legislature passed the dreadful nine-to-eight measures. At this time Alabama was filled with racial worries. The Freedom Riders, consisting of blacks and whites, were surging into Alabama, breaking law and order wherever they went. They had vowed to stamp out law, customs and traditions. They had malice against the South.

Alabama rebelled against the Freedom Riders, financed by Northern money. Headlines flared and gunfire hailed. "General" Bobby Kennedy moved in with federal marshals to enforce the law while at the same time he violated Alabama's law prohibiting federal intervention in state functions and rights, such as preserving law and order, unless asked.

At this critical time, Frank offered Congress legislation aimed at the Freedom Riders, who infested Alabama with civil rights. The Boykin measure would make it a federal offense to travel in interstate commerce with intent to violate state laws and incite a riot or commit any act or engage in any conduct that would cause a riot.

The Northern Democratic majority in the House would not give the South the safeguards. Crackdown on the South was the order of the day in Congress, the White House and the Supreme Court. Freedom Riders were out to change the states of the Old Confederacy.

Earlier, in January 1962, the House of Representatives forced a Cabinet-level Department of Urban Affairs and Housing upon a country already overburdened with bureaucracy. The House did not allow the bill that would transfer a vast program of centralized power to the federal government; the Kennedy administration already controlled the Rules Committee.

Beaten by the House, the president maneuvered to get the Cabinet agency by executive order. The move was crushed by an overwhelming vote in Congress to reject the president's proposal.

When Frank was in Mobile on business, he received a call from President Kennedy about another proposal facing rejection; this one was something Boykin supported.

"Frank," Kennedy said, "I need your help. It looks like we can't get enough votes to put the Farm Bill through the House."

Frank replied, "I'll do everything I can, Mr. President."

"Fine. I'll send my private plane down for you at once and have you here before morning."

"There's no need to do that, Mr. President. I can get a plane out of Mobile about midnight."

"Thanks, Frank. Call me tomorrow sometime."

Frank boarded the plane for Washington, arriving at 5:00 A.M. At Capitol Hill, administration leaders advised him they were ten votes shy of passing the Farm Bill.

"What do you suggest we do, Frank?"

He replied, "I only got here this morning and haven't had time to see my friends but give me ten days and we can put it through."

That morning, the House voted, and the bill lost by the predicted ten votes. Frank came out swinging and put it through on a reconsideration vote, by a margin of five.

The president was happy and phoned Frank, thanking him for a "grand job." It was more than "grand." It was superhuman.

CHAPTER TWENTY-ONE

The Black Day

In the preliminary, the nine-incumbent congressmen all won out, qualifying them for the statewide free-for-all that would eliminate one of their members. The people were the terminators and May 30 was D-day.

The incumbents began their final drive, traveling by bus, helicopter, plane and automobile. Frank cruised up and down the state seeking votes and running on his record: what he accomplished for his district in twenty-eight years.

Midway through Frank's campaign, he was summoned before the Grand Jury of Montgomery County, in Rockville, Maryland, which was probing the failure of savings and loan institutions in that area. He had an hour with the grand jurors and was quick with his wit. Passersby could hear the laughter from the jury room.

Frank stood his ground against any presumption of involvement in the tragic savings and loan fiasco. "Neither I nor any company in which I or any member of my family owns an interest has ever had any dealings with any savings and loan institutions in Maryland. I have nothing to hide. I have told the truth."

The Grand Jury of Montgomery County believed him and cleared him immediately.

Word got out instantly through newsprint and radio, and word of mouth was spread throughout the state. Jealousies of Frank were inflamed, and prejudice was enhanced. Innuendoes were flying that "Frank's too rich," or "He's too old," "He's too conservative," "He's too flamboyant," "His political ways are out of date," "He's mixed up in those terrible savings and loan failures in Maryland."

A reporter took offense that they stooped to the depths of ganging up on Frank because of his age. "What's wrong with age?" demanded an editor.

Hamner Cobbs of the Greensboro Watchman charged the Birmingham press with leadership in a North Alabama movement to engineer Frank's defeat. As May 30, approached, the city of Mobile was aware they might not have a congressman dedicated to her interests. Frank was in trouble and his campaign was running out of steam.

What could Mobile do? Not in 143 years of statehood had Alabama elected a governor from the state's Senate. It appeared she would lose her "very own" congressman.

The black day came: May 30, 1962, Memorial Day. Frank Boykin finished last out of the nine. It was his first defeat in twenty-seven years.

Capitol Hill was shocked and in disbelief. They hated losing a fixture in the House and at the Dome of the Capitol itself. Capitol Hill knew the good that Frank had done for Mobile and the rest of his district. He was a hardworking, flamboyant character who soared beyond state and national bounds, yet it seemed as if the state turned its back on its greatest worker and helper. Alabama would wait a long time before she found another who could be as successful in Washington.

Frank, being a good sport, bowed out graciously. He was a lame duck congressman with seven months to go until moving day. With his staff, he started packing up his priceless records: the reminders and photos of his twenty-seven years of labor on the Hill.

He continued wearing his bright smile and still sang, "Everything's Made for Love." "What am I going to do?" he beamed at an inquiring reporter. "I am going to work like a horse during the next seven months in Washington. I'll spend my time trying to get everything I can for this great state. While I regret for the people of this district that our efforts were not successful, I accept the decision of the voters of Alabama. The best interests of my district and state will be closest to my heart.

"I am naturally personally disappointed. I can only trust in what the Good Book says, 'All things work together for those who love the Lord.' God bless you all."

In the New York Times, Arthur Krock wrote the following:

And, come next session, the pleasingly corpulent, nonsmoking, nondrinking, jolly Boykin, with a heart as big as Minnie the Moocher's, but with a million or a billion in the bank just the same, will be absent from the chamber, the corridors, and the House barbershop of the Capitol.

The scene will be quieter. But who would rather have quiet than a continuous and thunderous assurance of universal love? A nut or something?

For Mobile, there were gloomy afterthoughts, dismay and counting the cost. The district was dismembered and her counties, including Mobile itself, would be parceled out like unneeded and unwanted stepchildren among the eight realigned districts—and not one of them were within a hundred and fifty miles of Mobile.

Well-wishers, friends, business associates, colleagues in the Senate and House and just plain folks sent Frank over 8,000 telegrams and letters bemoaning his loss. One such letter was from Clarence Cannon of Missouri, veteran chairman of the House Appropriations Committee and third-ranking member of the House in seniority, with nineteen terms serving Congress. His letter read:

Dear Frank:

I am shocked and distressed at the primary result from your great state.

I am certain I express the sentiments not only of your constituency, but of every member of the House and Senate when I deplore the developments which have brought about this unhappy situation.

Speaker Champ Clark, the greatest speaker in the history of the Congress, who led on every ballot in the national convention on thirty ballots for nomination for President of the United States when nomination meant certain election, had the same experience. He was so popular and so beloved that nobody ever dreamed there was a chance of his defeat. But, after all his distinguished service, notwithstanding the great respect and affection in which he was universally held in the District and the State and the Country, he was defeated by 8000 majority or more. The next morning after the election there wasn't a voter who was not astonished and dismayed at the defeat. If the election had been held the next day, he would have been elected by the greatest majority in the history of his district.

The trouble in both his and your case was that nobody dreamed he was in the slightest danger.

There can be no other explanation of the result of your primary. Everybody was certain you would be elected and concentrated on other candidates they thought might be in danger.

It is a national misfortune. But universal regret serves to emphasize the high esteem and affection in which you are held both here in Washington and at home.

With deepest regret and with warmest regard and best wishes,

Your friend,
Clarence Cannon

Congressman Boykin carried on business as usual for the seven months that were left of his service in the House. On July 2, in a thirty-minute speech praising President Kennedy's visit to Mexico, Frank touched on a matter that had tragic reminders. In part, he said:

Mr. Speaker, we are proud of our president of the United States, President John F. Kennedy; and we are proud of our president of Mexico, President Lopez Mateos. Why should not we be? Why should not all of the people of this great country be proud of the great day they had in Mexico City? Why should not all of our neighbors south of the border, in that great and marvelous Mexico, be proud? Surely, God had a hand in this great gathering in Mexico, where our president and his wife as well as his advisers gathered at a great feast of really and truly brotherly love.

I do not believe, Mr. Speaker, we have ever had a gathering just like this anywhere in the country. I have seen meetings, of course, here in the Capital of the United States, with all the greatest of the great—the same thing in New York and so many other places. But just to think—over one million of our neighbors, headed by their great president and his wife, and our group of Americans from Washington, who flew there for this great meeting, that, in my judgment, will mean so much, not only to our great nation just south of us: Mexico.

We had all sorts of threats when we learned that our president wanted to visit his neighbors, but that is the way the people who don't believe in God Almighty do—they bluff, and they try to do everything. I was talking to the men in the cloakroom here in Congress of the United States, and they said: 'What a pity that the president is going to go down there where he will take such a chance.' He was not taking any chance; he knew he was going there to do well, and the people in Mexico knew he was coming there to do well; as a matter of fact, they cannot because they have God on their side.

Well, it is great there, and, like here, we have now former President Herbert Hoover, former President Harry Truman, and former President Dwight D. Eisenhower—three great presidents—all living. I do not believe we ever before had four presidents in the United States living all at one time. Well, we need them all, and I believe every one of them are cooperating and doing what they can to help us. Mexico has the same thing—and they have some great men who have been president of that great country; and I am sure that every one of them, like the great President Aleman, are doing all in their power to get us closer together. It is for our good and their good and for the good of all mankind. So, God was guiding President Kennedy, Mrs. Kennedy, and their group when they went to visit our great neighbors, as the people used to do in the olden days that the Bible tells you about.

After his return from Mexico, President Kennedy received an unusual letter from the patriarch of the House, Carl Vinson of Georgia, then-chairman of the House Armed Services Committee. He wrote concerning the appointment of a successor to Abraham Ribicoff, secretary of Health, Education and Warfare, who was vacating his Cabinet post to pursue public office in his home state of Connecticut. Vinson wrote the following letter:

> *My dear Mr. President:*
>
> *I should like to take this opportunity to suggest to you a worthy successor to the very able Secretary of Health, Education, Welfare, who is leaving your Cabinet to seek public office in the State of Connecticut.*
>
> *Twenty-seven years ago, on July 30, 1935, the people of the First District of Alabama elected Frank W. Boykin to the 74th Congress to fill a vacancy caused by the resignation of his predecessor.*
>
> *For twenty-seven years this very capable, outstanding man has energetically and devotedly represented his constituents in the House of Representatives.*
>
> *Frank Boykin is an 'Old line' Democrat who has consistently and conscientiously placed the interest of his Nation and his Party above all other objectives.*
>
> *He is a living example of the opportunities that are available to all Americans who are willing to work.*
>
> *He has been an employee and an employer. He knows from firsthand experience the problems of the employee, and the problems of the employer.*
>
> *He has engaged in numerous business activities from real estate to lumber to live-stock to ship building. But he has also been a farmer.*
>
> *He knows what it is to work from early in the morning to late in the evening.*
>
> *He is the Horatio Alger of our day.*
>
> *He did not have the advantages of higher education; thus, he is fully aware of the importance of education.*

As a youth, he knew the problems of the poor; as a wealthy man, he knows the obligations of the well-to-do.

He has befriended literally thousands of his fellow Americans. His reputation as a humanitarian is unparalleled.

He fights for what he thinks is right; but he also understands and accepts the indispensability of teamwork.

I am thoroughly convinced that he would bring to your Cabinet, as Secretary of Health, Education and Welfare, the maturity of his vast experience, the imagination of unbounded energy, an insatiable drive for a better America, and a dignified respect for your outstanding leadership.

As you study the backgrounds and accomplishments of the many names that will be suggested to you to fill this position in your Cabinet, I commend to you Frank W. Boykin of Alabama. He is a man of intelligence, competence, loyalty, endearing personality, and dedicated to the expansion of a greater America.

I am convinced that Frank Boykin is a man who would be a dedicated and outstanding member of your official family.

Very respectfully yours,
Carl Vinson

October 3, 1962, the House abandoned its last-minute docket long enough to pay acclaim to public servant Frank W. Boykin. Frank was seated in the back of the House chamber, listening to the outpouring of admiration, enshrined in the Congressional Record.

Floor manager for the occasion was devoted friend L. Mendel Rivers of South Carolina, who would be succeeding to the chairmanship of the Armed Services Committee of the House. A few of the tributes paid to Frank by his colleagues were as follows:

Mr. McCormack: "Mr. Speaker, Frank Boykin and I have been very close friends during the period of years in which we have served together in the House of Representatives. Frank and Mrs. Boykin have lived, as have Mrs. McCormack and I for many years, at the Washington Hotel. Between Frank and Mrs. Boykin and John and Harriet McCormack there is a close friendship of many years, a friendship that we value very, very much.

"Mr. Speaker, Frank Boykin has been one of the hardest-working members of Congress during his many years of very important service in this body. He has certainly brought to Alabama and to the people of his district industry, credit, and honor. He is a man with an understanding mind which is without limitation, a man whose generosity and whose cheerfulness is known everywhere, a man who is universally respected by everyone who knows him.

"Mr. Speaker, I am very happy to join with my friend, the gentleman from South Carolina (Mr. Rivers) and his colleagues from Alabama in honoring this great man whose services in this body will no longer continue in the next Congress, but who during his years of service has made his mark in contributing to the legislative history of our country. He has always been prominent in nature, progressive in character, permanent and lasting in the legislative history of our country."

Mr. Rivers of South Carolina: "Mr. Speaker, I came to the Congress twenty-two years ago. My first good fortune was to meet Frank Boykin. The distinguished gentleman from Florida (Mr. Sikes) was one of the freshmen in that 77th Congress. By the stroke of good luck and good fortune, we met Frank Boykin. A close friendship has ensued from that day to this. It never occurred to me, nor has it occurred to you, that Frank Boykin would ever be defeated in the Congress of the United States, because he should not have been defeated. By the sad stroke of fortune, by the unpredictable turn of fortune's wheel, he was defeated. But he is really not defeated. He just did not make the grade under the conditions imposed by the State legislature.

"Mr. Speaker, already his departure from the Congress of the United States has cast affliction on this venerable body. When the 88th Congress convenes, and Frank Boykin is not here, this place will not be the same. His exuberance, his enthusiasms, his love, his friendliness for all his colleagues and for his fellow man pervades and pervaded and has permeated the loftiest rafter of this ageless parliamentary body.

"Mr. Speaker, Frank Boykin—it is not possible to use the English language and describe the character of this man. He is unique among men.

He is unique among public servants. When he will have left this Congress and departed this life, he will have been unique among all men. His kind flashes across the scene of life's stage only once in a thousand years. His impression will last as long as men of good will trod the venerable halls of this institution. Frank Boykin will never be forgotten as long as there is a Congress of the United States or as long as the archives of this country contain the efforts of men for their people.

"Mobile, Alabama, will certainly not be a desert in the field of representatives so long as Frank Boykin is there to voice her needs. As the distinguished gentleman from Florida has said, Frank Boykin has made Mobile the city it is. Without Frank Boykin there would be no Mobile, and without Frank Boykin a lot of Mobile would never have been heard from. You know this and I know this.

"He helped all people. He is known in your district, and he is known in mine because he had the time to help his colleagues. Our friendship, you know, and I know, is as full as possible. Our love and regard for each other will be a lasting as the sun in her journeys across the horizons.

"The memories of times I have had with Frank Boykin and the pleasure he has brought to this Hall with his cheer and his joy will remain as long as these walls stand. To know Frank Boykin was to love him.

"As has been said here today, he took time to do the little things. This marks a man of magnificent and astronomical stature. These are the things of which Frank Boykin is composed. Countless deeds too numerous to recall and which I am too feeble to describe and mark this great American. I shall never forget him. My life would not be the same and my activities would not be the same without him, because he helped me all the time. He was an institution; he was an inspiration to everybody who wants to work for the interests of the people of the nation he loves."

Mr. Grant: "Although denied the opportunity of a formal education, he has graduated with honors from the University of Hard Knocks. No one is more widely read than Frank nor has a better grasp of local, state, national, and international issues than he.

"Numbered among his many personal friends are those in high places, including presidents, the former prime minister of Great Britain, Winston Churchill, general of the Army, Douglas McArthur, General Issimo and Mrs. Chiang Kai-shek, and many other world leaders too numerous to mention. It can truly be said that 'He walks with kings yet keeps the common touch.' He has many faithful-colored employees on his hunting reservation in Alabama who dearly love him. After their retirement, they do not have to worry about social security or other benefits as 'Mr. Frank' looks after their every need. A friend in need is a friend; indeed, he has been just that type friend to many people.

"No one in Congress is better known than he. With his jovial smile and waving arms as he goes happily along, saying a cheerful 'hi' to everyone he meets, one cannot help but be charmed by his outgoing, friendly manner.

"Several times on the floor of the House in private conversation, I have heard Frank say, 'Isn't it a shame that we have so much bickering and misunderstandings and wouldn't it be a wonderful thing if we could have a lighted cross on the wall above the Speaker's rostrum?' So, I know that was gratifying to him when the House just a few days ago passed a resolution authorizing that the inscription 'In God We Trust' be placed over the Speaker's desk."

With many other commemorations given that day, Frank was at a loss for words over all the kind remarks and found it hard to hold back the tears of joy.

From the White House came a last-minute salutation: "You can take just pride in your years of service in the Congress of the United States. Your contribution to the nation and to your constituency should be a constant source of satisfaction to you."

On October 16, Congress adjourned, and Frank doffed the toga he had worn for twenty-seven years. He left graciously with no fanfare. Tom Donnelly, columnist for the *Washington Daily News*, wrote: "Many men would give ten years off their lives merely to dip a toe into such a bath (of praise) .... Of this man who built his political career on the slogan 'Everything's Made for Love' it seems only fitting to concede that Washington is losing a solon, and Alabama is regaining a sun."

The next day, Frank and Ocllo boarded a plane for Mobile with devastatingly bad news. A federal Grand Jury in Baltimore had indicted Frank and his friend, Representative Thomas Johnson of Maryland, for conspiracy and conflict of interest in real estate transactions involving both congressmen. He felt weak at the knees at hearing the news. It was impossible to imagine how a man who'd kept such exemplary records, with ledgers going back to 1918, could get into such trouble. Yet Frank's sole comment to the press, as he led Ocllo into the plane, was, "I am innocent of any wrongdoing."

The press was having a field day with the news. At Birmingham Airport, Boykin was met with an onslaught of reporters. When a staff writer for a newspaper asked if he intended to return to Maryland and face trial, Frank exploded: "Yes, sir! Hell, yes!"

Waiting to welcome Frank and Ocllo in Mobile were family and friends. From his home later that night, he issued the following statement: "I did not know anything about the charges against me until today when I was leaving Washington to return home by plane after having attended my final session of Congress. I deny again that I am guilty of any wrongdoing. When I have seen all the charges against me, I will see that all the facts are brought out and my name cleared, and my position vindicated. I have come home to enjoy my family and friends."

He went to Washington, as he told Edward Boykin, "Not for pleasure or for profit, but to build my district." After his departure from Congress in 1962, an audit of his non-reimbursed expenses revealed that during his twenty-eight years of service, he had spent a million dollars more than he had received from the government. His personal wealth was concentrated in land the day he entered Congress in 1935 and he owned more then than when he left in 1962.

Frank was a multi-millionaire, owning over eighteen businesses, ranging from shipbuilding to the queen bee industry, throughout his life. His timber ventures were running at great guns. So, the congressional salary of seventy-five hundred dollars a year, with an allowance of twenty-five hundred for office help and expenses, was no great inducement for him to serve. A comparison that Frank would later draw in 1964 summed it up: "I have made more money in a month since I have gotten out of Congress than I made during the entire twenty-eight years I was there."

However, he insisted that a congressman—enacting legislation affecting nearly two hundred million Americans—should be compensated accordingly with a yearly remuneration of at least fifty thousand dollars a year. Throughout his lengthy service, his monthly telephone bill far exceeded his government pay.

* * *

The night after his arrival in Mobile, at a twenty-five-dollar-a-plate dinner, there was a proclamation of "Frank Boykin Day." It was a way for the Mobile government and citizens to make amends by giving him a gala. The city presented him the "Mobile Citizen's Award" and over 2,000 citizens signed a scroll to him. It helped a little bit with the hurt feelings that remained of not having gotten the votes for the man who did so much for Mobile.

George Wallace was at the "Frank Boykin Day" dinner and made a speech. Frank thought he was a great man and was for him in both elections because he was a fighter and had guts, he was a good American, and Frank felt he would make the best governor they'd ever had.

The *Indianapolis Star* wrote:

> *Frank Boykin has become a sort of political legend both in Washington and Alabama. American politics will probably be able to withstand the loss of such a colorful character.... The real tragedy is the fact that Mobile, Alabama, a city of more than two hundred thousand, and the old First District of that State, will have no spokesman in Congress...*

A new public figure became a gubernatorial candidate and won the election. George Wallace had pledged that if he became governor, he would appoint the low man in the nine-to-eight primaries as the governor's personal representative in Washington, as a sort of representative-at-large. Frank was the perfect man for the job.

Frank never gave the impression he would return to his old role on Capitol Hill. But he would assume whatever role in Washington that was necessary to perform.

CHAPTER TWENTY-TWO

Burglaries

A burglary of Frank's home on Monterey Street in Mobile, Alabama, occurred on the memorable night of March 5, 1962. Police were called and the report stated it was a professional craftsman. Entry was achieved through the large French doors that opened onto the front porch, yet no piece of the bric-a-brac on a table just inside was out of place.

Frank and Ocllo were in Washington that month as Congress was in session. The crooks picked a Mardi Gras carnival night. The time of year, Mobile came alive, and most citizens were enjoying the merriment of music, revelry and parades; it was the perfect time to burglarize the Boykin home. They could not have picked a better night.

The day before the robbery, an anonymous man phoned the Boykin home. The maid, Martha, who was the nanny for forty-six years of service to the Boykins, answered the phone.

"Are the congressman and his wife in town?"

"No, they're in Washington, but I expect them home in a few days," replied Martha.

"Do you stay in the house at night?"

"No, I'm just leaving now, but I come in several times a week to dust a little and see that things are all right."

The next morning, at about seven, Martha entered the house and knew immediately it had been robbed. In hysterics, she ran next door to the neighbors and Mrs. Ogden opened the door, with Martha anxiously saying, "The Boykins' house has been broken into during the night."

Mrs. Ogden volunteered that when she went to bed around midnight, she thought she heard noises in the Boykin house. Her suspicions were so aroused that she turned on her yard light.

The detectives found no clues or fingerprints with a diligent search and examination of the premises. Silverware and valuable jewelry worth thousands of dollars were untouched. The master bedroom was ransacked and the lock to a huge wardrobe was sawed out so neatly and replaced that the circular scar was barely noticeable. Inside the wardrobe were several large drawers with locks that were jimmied open. The contents were scattered everywhere on the floor, with mementos, baby curls, old love letters and many keepsakes, none of which the vandals wanted.

Upon examination, the mantle in the room had been torn apart with a fine-toothed electric saw, pried out and replaced. From deductive reasoning, the police and family believed they were after incriminating papers, of which there were none. The burglars continued ruining much of the furniture, looking for hidden crypts. Dozens of pictures on the wall were destroyed, with the backs torn off and tossed away for nothing. Hundreds of papers were found scattered and tattered throughout the rooms and halls. Many, many books were taken from the bookcases and shaken out for what might have contained concealed papers.

"They must have been in the house for hours," commented Frank later. "They were very reckless. For instance, we have some very fine trunks we brought back from Hong Kong. They have all sorts of things in them, and they have complicated brass locks. They broke into all these, investigating everything in them. For instance, forty years ago at Palm Beach we had a party for President Harding, who was an old friend of mine, and we saved some of the absinthe from that party. We used it at the weddings of our granddaughters. We also had in there some old papers from the old Ku Klux Klan trial that framed about fifty Mobile citizens, including myself. The case was thrown out of court. They also took one of my pistols, and a good one at that.

"Not only did they break into our home at Mobile, but they rifled our rooms at the Emerson Hotel in Baltimore during my Baltimore trial, and they were looking for papers which I would have gladly handed them if I had them," said Frank.

Frank and his office staff had sent the federal attorney all the letters and books showing where he bought the land in question, the price of the land and what county seat it was recorded in, as well as the income taxes he paid on it. "The burglars preferred to pillage our rooms, invading our privacy, even with us absent. They must have been desperate, as they broke into my automobile that I used during the trial. They twice ransacked my office in the House Office Building."

* * *

At this point in reading the records, Grace looked up at her father and asked, "Who were 'they'?"

Bob replied, "We thought we knew who sent the robbers, but couldn't prove it. The phones were tapped for months before my father's trial and while it was going on."

"Who ordered the police-state methods to get evidence to convict Frank?" Grace continued.

"He had said he thought of only one crowd that was searching high and low for evidence to send him to prison," Bob replied.

Grace's eyes went wide with curiosity as she delved back into the documents—and back in time

* * *

When Attorney General Robert Kennedy moved to New York, he left behind accusations that he had employed unlawful undercover methods to get evidence that convicted teamster boss Jimmy Hoffa. In December 1965, a committee of the United States Senate was probing into wiretapping and bugging operations of the Justice Department. The committee just skimmed the surface, with Robert Kennedy being a senator from the Empire State. Of course, the politicians' "club" is very protective of its own.

Whoever pirated Frank's home, offices and car had been given an 'unrestricted hunting license' to bring Frank down. They used electronic and other technical aids, as well as such investigative techniques as surveillance, undercover work, etc., including burglary. The politically motivated raids on the Boykins was never broadcast or noted by the national media in 1962, but it could have helped lead to the backdrop of the scandals that developed into Watergate.

On October 29, 1965, Drew Pearson of the *Washington Post* stated, "The man who really started the eavesdropping was none other than Bobby Kennedy when he was Attorney General."

None of these points were bought up during the trial against Frank and his family to the jury that tried him!

* * *

At this moment, Grace looked up again, exasperated. "What was the trial all about?"

Her father replied, "It all started in 1953 when my dad bought two tracts of timberland, one near Brooke, Virginia, and the other adjoining Waldorf, Maryland, for the benefit of the Tensaw Land & Timber Company and the Washington Lumber and Turpentine Company he founded years before."

"So, Tensaw Land & Timber Company, which we still own today, was involved?" Grace asked.

"Yes, that's why the family was involved, because all of those involved with Tensaw was a part. The Maryland property consisted of eight thousand acres, with the one in Virginia having five thousand. They were within thirty minutes driving time of the nation's capital and had opportunities for great profit. Dad had such insight in real estate operations for fifty years, which made him a millionaire. Buying acreage in large blocks was old hat for him. He'd purchased and sold millions of acres and large and small 'trades' by this time in his life. The Waldorf tract was larger than the District of Columbia and probably the largest underdeveloped single tract of land in the state of Maryland.

"Frank built his fortune on the development and exploitation of land, its timber and natural resources, not only in Alabama, Florida, and other states, but in Mexico as well. But the main attractions of those two tracts of land were timber, sand and gravel, and their subdivision possibilities were to accommodate the exploding housing needs of nearby Washington.

"In 1962," Bob continued, "the newspapers and other media's headline stories were the unregulated Maryland savings and loan associations.

There were many tales of outsiders who had come into the state and collaborated with local politicians who milked money from the public, used some of the money in questionable real estate project and put money into their pockets. The Washington Post had a crusade aimed at all people that had anything to do with the savings and loans association. Remember, Frank was a Southern congressman from the state of Alabama, where Governor Wallace had stood at the school door opposing federal intervention while blacks demanded their civil rights. And the Kennedy name carried such weight that the family itself was becoming a dynasty."

"So, what are you saying, Dad?" Grace wondered.

"The basis of the indictment involved the unregulated savings and loan associations in Maryland and the two large tracts of land that were owned by Frank's family-owned corporation. The big players in the suit were the Honorable John F. Kennedy, as president of the United States; the Honorable Robert F. Kennedy, as attorney general; the Honorable Joseph P. Kennedy, as former ambassador to the Court of St. James and a close, personal friend of Frank's; the Honorable Joseph D. Tydings, as counsel for the prosecution and campaign manager for John F. Kennedy for the State of Maryland, subsequently appointed U.S. district attorney for Maryland and also running for Senate; the Honorable Thomas F. Johnson, a member of Congress from the First District of the State of Maryland, who was publicly known for his aspirations for a seat in the Senate; and Edward Bennett Williams, Esquire, attorney for Frank and one of the most noted defendant counsels in the United States. The Grand Jury was composed of black and white men and women from the Baltimore area.

"The *Washington Post* was closely aligned to the Kennedy administration and made the headlines about the Maryland savings and loan associations, and about my father and Congressman Johnson, for many months before the indictment and during the trial.

"Of course, Dad had many accolades for his life and businesses. Those closest to him know he would do anything for anyone, whether it was a telephone operator, a chairwoman in an office building, a hotel clerk, the president of the United States, or the highest rank in the military service. He was so generous and would help anyone..."

"Even to his own detriment," Grace concluded.

Bob nodded and continued his story. "At the end of 1960, Frank met J. Kenneth Edlin, who told him he was in the financing business and wanted to help Frank's friends. Dad introduced him to the owners of the housing project, who attempted to work out a financing program. The financing took months, and it finally came out in conversation with Frank that Edlin had been indicted under a mail fraud charge in the Federal District Court in Baltimore, but the indictment was unfair.

"Your grandfather called his good friend Bobby Kennedy, who was then attorney general. Frank and Joe Kennedy were long-time friends, Dad served in Congress with John Kennedy, he knew the entire family on a first-name basis and had even entertained them. So, he had Bobby inquire into the Edlin mail fraud case. This is one of the letters he sent to Bobby."

Grace took the letter her father handed her and started to read:

My Dear Bob:

I ran into our mutual, beloved dear friend Congressman Tom Johnson last night when we passed the President Depressed Areas Bill by a real majority. For some reason or other, Tom had never met you and he was so impressed with you and your great work and the courtesies you extended to us when we visited you last Saturday. He told me that he was more determined than ever to help put your great brother's program into law. I thought I would just pass this information along to you. It was really a great day in the Capitol here yesterday where we passed by a real majority three different, great and good programs and Tom Johnson and his entire Maryland group worked like Trojans. I would like to also tell you that our mutual dear friend, Governor Luther Hodges, now great Secretary of Commerce, was right out there buttonholing the boys and I am sure the President, you and your famous, fabulous father and all your family must be mighty happy about the great work we all did for Easter.

I think the President handled the Laos situation in a masterful way, and how I hope all of you will have a good Easter, especially that little human dynamo wife of yours who we think is so wonderful in every way and the same goes for you and all of your great family now and always.

God bless you and yours, now and forever, sincerely your friend,

Frank W. Boykin

When she was finished, her father added, "Attorney general's answers to the letters Frank sent to him were remarkably crisp, short and almost curt...not warm at all."

"Well, they *are* from Massachusetts," Grace joked, trying to bring a little levity to the situation.

Her father smiled then continued. "Your grandfather, not being an attorney, relied on the Justice Department to advise him on this matter. Over several months there were several meetings and telephone conversations with Frank, Bobby, Tom Johnson and Bobby's assistants. They told Frank the charges against Edlin had merit and should be tried, and that he should refrain from any more contact with officials of the Department of Justice.

"The financing arrangements that Edlin tried to make with the owners of the land in Charles County didn't work out. Edlin went to Frank to have his family corporation sell him the mortgage with the terms of having the payments made over twice the number of years called for in the original mortgage. He didn't waste his breath, talking your grandfather into the terms, which proved to be bad for the family-owned corporation that owned the mortgage.

"Edward Bennett Williams repeatedly stated the fact during the trial that Frank was on the short end of the deal and the family corporation lost a lot with Edlin's companies. The Boykins' family-owned corporation sold five thousand acres of land in Virginia to one of Edlin's controlled companies for a small down payment and a long-term payout. During both transactions, Frank was told by Edlin that the corporations made purchases composed by a group of investors from Chicago, New York and Miami, which were not Edlin's companies. Later, during the trial, Frank learned of the corporations that were Edlin's. He realized at that time the funds of Edlin's Maryland chartered savings and loan associations had entered his two land projects. Not one penny ever exchanged hands or went into Frank's pocket personally in any of the transactions!"

Grace shook her head sadly as her father went on.

"Congressman Johnson, who had a law firm that did some legal work on behalf of Edlin's companies, introduced Frank to Edlin. So, it was the prosecution's attempt to show that Frank benefitted personally from an alleged agreement to intervene with the Justice Department on Edlin's behalf, and that Johnson did, too, with the fees paid to his law firm used as payments to him, as a congressman, for such intervention. Accounts in newspapers were repeated, along with stories of how the maze of intricate savings and loan transactions were confusing to many of the experts. The members of the Grand Jury or the trial jury couldn't fully realize what it was that Frank was accused of or what he was convicted of. Even the well-known Edward Bennett Williams was dismayed that Frank had no understanding at all of what he was being tried for or how he could be convicted. Still, the prosecution continued its effort to make out that the tracts of land involved were worthless and that Edlin paid an inflated price for them. Appraisers were brought into court to claim they were merely swamps, impossible to develop."

"Don't those same lands today have government-guaranteed loans of up to twenty-seven million dollars? And aren't there more than three thousand houses and well over twenty-five thousand residents in the community developments at St. Charles, Maryland?" Grace asked, outraged.

"That's true," her father agreed. "But the prosecution ignored the point that Virginia land was one of the better-known developments in the state. In fact, the current owners recently sold over five million dollars worth of lots. Here...look at this."

Bob handed Grace an article by the *Baltimore People's* Tom Kelly, with the headline: "*A Letter to Bobby from Boykin—You're Great; So's Your Old Man.*"

Grace read:

> *Baltimore, April 12, Former Congressman Frank W. Boykin is a man of letters, long, effusive letters that rival the richest ingredients in Little Orphan Annie, Sonnets from the Portuguese, or a TV commercial.*

> Mr. Boykin, ex congressman Thomas F. Johnson, of Maryland, ex savings & loan magnate J. Kenneth Edlin and William Robinson, an attorney, are all on trial in Federal Court.
>
> They are charged with trying vainly to influence the Justice Department on Edlin's behalf.
>
> Yesterday, after seven days devoted mainly to the other three defendants, the Government got around to Mr. Boykin, his life and his letters.
>
> **LETTERS READ**
>
> U.S. Atty. Joseph Tydings read half a dozen of the letters to the jury in clear but undramatic voice. Perhaps he felt they spoke best for themselves.
>
> The richness of Mr. Boykin's style is difficult to express in any words other than his own. Consider this gentle note to Atty. General Robert F. Kennedy..."

Grace paused. "This is the same letter to RFK that you just handed me a copy of a minute ago."

"That's right," Bob Boykin said.

Grace skipped ahead then continued reading:

> **OTHER LETTERS**
>
> There were other letters to the Attorney General in which Mr. Boykin genially referred to "your marvelous mother" and "your great family" and one in which he invited the entire Kennedy clan to dinner on the Starlight Roof.
>
> It is almost embarrassing to note that the Attorney General's answers to the letters tended to be remarkably crisp and singularly undemonstrative.
>
> Mr. Boykin's other spotlighted correspondent yesterday was Henry Holland, of Mobile, accountant for the Boykin family firm, Tensaw Land and Lumber Co. A faithful writer, Mr. Boykin once sent two letters covering a total of six and a half single spaced pages to Mr. Holland in one day. The letters

covered the bewildering details of multi-million-dollar land deals involving Mr. Boykin, Mr. Johnson, and Edlin.

They also covered the touching gift of some Hereford cattle to Mr. Johnson. We had best resort again to the man's own words:

"...In the deal, as I told you, I think, Mr. Edlin agreed to give Congressman Tom Johnson who brought us together, some cows, provided I would furnish the bull..."

Most of the big deals never came to pass but the small one worked out fine. Mr. Johnson got the cows and Mr. Boykin furnished the bull.

Grace cleared her throat. "At the twilight of Frank's life, he had to bear a cross that few people in the prime of their lives could have stood. Why? Was it because he was a Southern congressman during the time the civil rights movement reacted against Southern elected officials being tried in a criminal proceeding? Or was it the relentless newspaper publicity and the political ambitions of others? Either way, it's inconceivable that a man of his stature could have had a totally impartial trial."

"You're right," Bob stated. "And after the jury read its verdict in July 1963, Frank was given a fine of forty thousand dollars in lieu of any sentence. This was a small amount of money, considering his wealth. Then Lyndon Johnson became president, and with the recommendation of Attorney General Bobby Kennedy, a full and complete presidential pardon was given to him. It should never have happened in the first place. But at least he received complete restoration of all rights and vindication in the eyes of family and friends."

"Look at this," Grace said, rifling through the documents. "On Wednesday, December 22, 1965, *The Kansas City Times* wrote this article..."

L.B.J. Grants Boykin Pardon
Alabama ex-Congressman was convicted in Fraud Case. Head of Timber firm Dixie Democrat, 80, suffering from a Heart Condition.

Washington (AP)—President Johnson has granted a pardon to Frank W. Boykin, 80, the former Alabama congressman convicted of conspiracy to defraud the United States in violating conflict of interest laws. He had been accused of attempting to influence the Justice department in handling mail fraud charges in savings and loan case.

The pardon, disclosed yesterday, was signed by the President last Friday and made effective as of Monday.

The Justice department said the Democratic former House member, now head of a timber firm in Alabama, has a serious heart condition and suffers from high blood pressure.

Boykin was fined $40,000.00 and sentenced to six months probation after he was convicted on eight counts in the U.S. District court in Baltimore October 7, 1963. Boykin was not given a prison sentence in view of his age and physical condition. The effect of the pardon is to clear his record and restore his civil rights he lost at the time of his conviction.

Boykin, reached by telephone at his Mobile office, said, "I'm very happy. I just learned of the pardon today.

"I thought all along that right would prevail," Boykin said, "and now it has."

The former congressman is still very active. He said his lumber business has doubled since he left Congress. "We workday and night," he said. Boykin is chairman of the board of Tensaw Land & Timber Company. His sons and daughter now do most of the work in running the business, Boykin said. The firm has been in business since 1900.

Boykin, who said his future plans consisted of building his business even bigger, expressed hope that he would get back the $40,000.00 he paid in connection with the fraud case.

He said he understood that since he had received a full and unconditional pardon, his fine would be returned.

Also convicted was former Rep. Thomas F. Johnson (D-Md.), who was sentenced to six months in jail and a $5,000.00 fine but whose conviction was reversed by a court appeal. The

> *government is now appealing that reversal before the Supreme Court.*
>
> *Three senators and 34 House members, comprising most of the delegations from Alabama, Florida, Mississippi and South Carolina, wrote in support of Boykin.*
>
> *The two congressmen were tried with J. Kenneth Edlin, operator of a savings and loan associate, William Robertson.*
>
> *The government charged Edlin and Robertson with mail fraud and accused Johnson of having accepted money to make speeches on their behalf in the House. Boykin and Johnson also were accused of attempting to use their influence on behalf of the two men with Justice Department officials.*

After hearing of her grandfather's trial, Grace continued to sift through thousands of papers and millions to possibly billions of words about Frank Boykin—and from his own mouth—that documented his life well lived.

Along with others of the family's third and fourth generations, she feels as though the conviction was a travesty of justice and a quest for an honorable man's execution. The heart condition Frank had before the indictment flared up during the trial, and on the advice of his doctors, consistent with that of his trial counsel, Edward Bennett Williams, he was not allowed to appeal the verdict since everyone who played a part felt it would endanger the great man's life.

Bob Boykin quoted his father as saying, "Even Jesus, in picking only twelve disciples, had one traitor." But Frank made it through his anguish with characteristic cheerfulness, hard work and friendship toward all who crossed his path.

CHAPTER TWENTY-THREE

End of an Era of 'Love' in Congress

Thursday, September 28, 1967, Proceedings and Debates of the 99th Congress, First Session. Congressional Record. A Tribute to Two Leaders.

Mr. Sikes, Mr. Speaker, Frank Boykin has been away from our midst for a few years. However, the memory is in the hearts of those who were privileged to serve with him. He was a great Congressman, who ably represented Alabama and the Nation. He and his sweet and lovely wife, Ocllo, are indeed among the very finest of people. Frank is a big man physically and a big man mentally, but his heart is the biggest thing about him. Recently he sent to me an article about Ed Ball, outstanding Florida industrialist, and Frank's good friend of many years. It was Frank's thought that this article, which involves an important side of Ed Ball, should be printed in the Congressional Record. Ed Ball's achievements are indeed monumental, and these things should be better known. It occurs to me that Frank Boykin's letter, which is so typical of the man, would also make fascinating reading. According to I submit both...

This is an excerpt of the Congressional Record to show how many years later Frank Boykin was still very much respected and missed.

There is also quotes from today's times form people who personally knew Frank W. Boykin:

November 13, 2008: "During the late '50s, around 1959, Mr. Frank, Joe Middleton and Paul Murray were going to Mobile in Mr. Frank's black Cadillac. We were near Katie Boykin Club when Mr. Frank said to Joe that there was gold out there. We drove a little way further and I asked Mr. Frank if gold was buried back there and he said, 'No, son, those pine trees are.'" Paul Murray of Jackson, Alabama, also said: "Brookley Field, Scott Paper Company and International Paper would not be closed if Mr. Frank was still living today!"

Bob Boykin, Frank's son, said, "He was a dynamic father that carried his own ball. He made fortunes and today he would be in the top ten of richest men. He had a lot of land in Waldorf, Maryland, but the population prevented him from developing it. He would be a Buffett if he lived today. Now, the right people get the right people to get things done. He helped poor and everyone. He's a dynamic man without a cruel streak in his body. He was always greeting his friends, politicians, constituents and family with a 'Howdy, pardner, everything is made for love.' He had a witty tongue. Once while he appeared before a House agriculture subcommittee, he announced that he had been attacked by fire ants in a most 'vulnerable spot' while sitting on a stump in Alabama. 'It would be a shame,' he announced, 'if we spent all our money fighting communists and then got destroyed by fire ants.' Regardless of the problem, he would always seem to rise above the situation."

Bob also said that Frank's personal motto that he learned for himself, perhaps from watching his mother and father, was: "Integrity in taking care of family. Showing respect to all people and being good to those that work around you."

"He could do no wrong. He was revered by all that knew him as a man of his word," said Mrs. Alice Miller Lewis of Sweet Water, Alabama, on March 7, 2009.

"Everybody's friend. He will always be remembered for his twenty-minute naps and he always replied, 'I'll be good to go.' He predicted industry from Pine Hill to Mobile, Alabama," said Harry A. Mason, mayor of Pine Hill, Alabama, on March 7, 2009.

Reverend Bobby Rene, minister at St. Stephen Baptist Church, said that, in the late 1960s, Frank visited his home next to the church. Frank was a guest of a doctor who was speaking at the church and, that afternoon, needed a nap. He sat down and said, "I'll sleep here on the couch," and so he did. This story was told throughout the years and "was a once in a lifetime experience for this family," said Jackie Rene on December 9, 2008, at White Smith Memorial Library in Jackson, Alabama.

Sentimentalists often forget the impermanent nature of politics, which the multi-millionaire, seventy-seven-year-old Frank never forgot. He was an exponent of having a super-abundant life, secure as the Capitol Dome and twice as expansive.

"Dad," Grace asked her father when they reached the very last file cabinet full of papers. "Do you remember the poem I wrote as a teenager called 'A Sentiment'?"

"Yes," Bob said. "Wait here. I saved it for you in my mementos." He left the room and came back a few minutes later holding the poem, which he read aloud to his daughter:

A Sentiment

Standing at the unknown year and facing the days ahead.
I trust you may meet all they hold in store. With composure one lifts their heads.
I hope this will be your most gratifying year in trying to do the greatest good.
Tiresomely, we are doing the greatest good for the largest number of people.
Today the wall that can't be scaled may reveal a door to let you through.
The soil produced from stones may grow. The life you sought for, Sick at heart.
He rises to greet you, like the dawn, around the corner—face to face.
So, keep on—keeping on!
As custodians with vast acres of God's beautiful land, we take great pride in his wild creatures.

> To me there is nothing more beautiful than the sheen on a turkey's wing in sunlight, and the leaves with multicolored variations in the season of the Fall.
> The natural things to me are the beautiful things as words are a vehicle of expression. They are wonderful tools to work with. The perfect carving, molding and ordering of words is a special gift of God.
> Words are the Heartstrings and the Harp on which we play, awakening laughter, tears and compassion and Displeasure, yielding, desire, and feeling of anxiety.
> Not many merciless words are said but I am one that has used them. Words that cut like a two-edged sword, straight to the ear.
> But prefer the contact of thought putting your hand in the tint of the multihued rainbow with something drawn of its loveliest aspects of color.
>
> —Written by Grace Boykin

* * *

The congressman had to run at large for the eight seats available after a reapportionment squeeze. The man was a legend for his twenty-eight years; he stood for "Love" and ended up a very low man on Alabama's political totem pole.

His battle cry was "Everything's Made for Love," and that made him famous. Huge banners proclaimed the motto and hung at every one of his meetings, and it was virtually impossible not to notice his prominence in his office.

No matter the time of day or night, chances were that Frank Boykin would greet strangers and friends alike with a gregarious approach—and that "Everything's Made for Love" would find its way into the conversation. Even in defeat, the Alabama politician still put in days that would exhaust many much younger than he. He usually started with a tremendous roar for coffee at 5:00 a.m. and then would dictate a few twenty-page letters on an infinite variety of subjects. As readers can see in this book, some of his letters were quite lengthy.

He would often invite officials to his seventeen-thousand-acre hunting preserve in McIntosh, Alabama, along with making casual references to the problems of the day. After his dictating, he would have a breakfast of fruit, eggs, hotcakes, grits, ham, biscuits and coffee. He would go on to 'never meet a stranger' after breakfast.

Frank Boykin would enter a room and it was as if a thousand butterflies were turned loose. He was nearly six feet tall, weighed more than 200 pounds and dressed elegantly in statesman attire, always making him look like a congressman. His white hair flowing back from a full face distinguished him from many others.

Mr. Boykin's office could be described as a political Noah's Ark, for the rooms contained photos of the rich and famous, all dedicated to the congressman. He had two huge rattlesnake skins, five mounted deer heads, a nine-foot wolf hide, old campaign posters and snapshots of hound dogs at work. The tables and cabinet of his so-called 'private' office were loaded with curios, trophies, antiques and mementos. He had a large cuckoo clock from Germany's Black Forest, two six-shooters that once belonged to Jesse James, a machete, assorted rifles and a chastity belt; walking into his office was like walking into a museum.

Frank was famous for his party-giving, and one that is especially notable was for Speaker of the House Sam Rayburn, with nearly a thousand friends in attendance. They served salmon, elk, venison, bear steaks, turkey and opossum, with lots to drink.

The speeches he made to the House floor included his annual orations on the widening of the Tombigbee River in his native Alabama to accommodate ocean-going vessels. Even though the house operated on the five-minute rule for speeches, they would let Frank talk on and on.

During his twenty-eight years in the House, Frank was a conservative and a loved congressman. At age eighty-four, he died of a heart attack at George Washington Hospital. He was eulogized as having traveled his life in "unique splendor." And no congressman has ever had a greater love for the First District of Alabama than Frank W. Boykin did. His motto lives on with his family today: "Everything's Made for Love."

At the table with her father, Grace read out loud one sample letter that followed Frank's passing:

United States Senate
Washington, D.C. 20510
Spessard L. Holland
Florida
March 14, 1969

Dear Mrs. Boykin:
I am deeply distressed because of the passing of your husband, Frank. He was one of the most generous and most loyal persons that I have ever known, and he will be missed by literally thousands of friends.
Asking that you accept my sympathy, in which Mary joins me, for yourself and other members of your family, I remain
Yours faithfully,
Spessard L. Holland

Dr. Joel D. McDavid, minister of Dauphin Way United Methodist Church in Mobile, Alabama, delivered this memorial message, which could not go unwritten:

The Honorable Frank W. Boykin March 14, 1969
We are all pilgrims, sojourners here; the earth is not a permanent dwelling place—not for any of us. For some it is a long journey beginning as delight spreads its brightness like the wings of morning. When the sun makes its appearance, the traveler is far lost to a colorful glow of the horizon. Not very long thereafter, night has come, and the journey has ended—such is the story of life. It is a bit more than a figure of speech; the description is more accurate.
The one hundred and twenty-first Psalms describes something of life's journey; it would be well for us to hear the Psalmist as he speaks:
"The Lord is thy keeper; the Lord is thy shade upon thy right hand. The sun shall not smite thee by day, nor the moon by night. The Lord shall preserve thee from all evil; he shall preserve thy soul. The Lord shall preserve thee from all evil; he

shall preserve the soul. The Lord shall preserve thy going out and thy coming in from this time forth and even forevermore."

We travel not in solitude, nor is our safety and our care dependent upon our weak skills nor our frail strength. With us and preserve us. How much richer a journey is when we have an interesting and helpful companion. It can reach supreme joy because God is that companion.

Some hasten on the journey; they rush to their destination, see no primroses along the way and chat with new friends; they have no time for a helping hand, a cheerful greeting, an encouraging word—they miss the joy of it all!

Today we assemble in this holy place to memorialize one whose journey was marked with unique splendor—Frank Boykin, congressman, business executive, leader of men, is known by all as "Frank" or some friendly title which identified him with men. He lived by hard work and a crowded schedule, but always had time for people. The hosts who gather here and thousands of others who mourn with us in this hour, give clear testimony to his capacity for friendship. He knew how to be a friend to men; in marble halls of splendor and in cottages of simplicity, he had time for friendship.

His hands were busy producing; his mind at work investing and re-investing; he was never too busy, however, to help. No congressman was more anxious to serve his constituency in a personal way; no favor was too small to escape his personal attention. Mobile and the First District enjoy the things and prosperity because of his helping hand.

While on his journey he was joyous and optimistic. One thinks of the joyous storytellers in Chaucer's Canterbury Tales, or the singers on a religious pilgrimage. Frank Boykin made his mission in life to lift the depressed, bring encouragement to the downhearted, to spread joy instead of gloom. Life has been made so much brighter by his having traveled this way.

Accompanying him on this journey, as is true with us all, is the God of all life. Frank knew this and claimed this presence as the source of this happy, helpful, hard-working life. He said,

"Everything is made for love!" and we smiled... Until we hear him complete the statement—"because God is love."

The journey is not ended—not at all. It moves on beyond the sunset into God's eternity—"The Lord shall preserve thy going out and thy coming in, from this time forward and even forevermore."

Who can describe life after death and who can paint its magnificence on a canvass? We do not know what eternity is, but we know God who made it, so we rest our cases as did Whittier:

I know not what the future hath
Of marvel or surprise
Assured alone that life and death
His mercy underlies.

And so, beside the silent sea
I wait the muffled oar
No harm from him can come from me
On ocean or on shore.

I know not where His islands lift
Their fronded palms in air
I only know I cannot drift
Beyond His love and care.

Each probate judge, sheriff and the clerk and registrar of the Circuit Court is required by law to preserve this slip or pamphlet in a book kept in his or her office until act is published in permanent form:

ALABAMA LAW
(Special Session, 1969)

Act No. 67 H.J.R. 15—Collins (C), Perloff, Marr, Collins (W), Grayson, Downing, Nettles, Lyons, Edington,

Wood

HOUSE JOINT RESOLUTION

WHEREAS former Congressman Frank W. Boykin passed away on March 12, 1969, and

WHEREAS Frank W. Boykin will be missed by hundreds of friends throughout Alabama and the entire United States, and the entire public has lost a dear friend, and

WHEREAS, Frank W. Boykin was born in Choctaw County, Alabama, and started his business career at the age of eight by carrying water for a railroad gang and was considered a business tycoon in his teens, and by the time he was first elected to Congress in 1935 he had gained a widespread reputation in the business world with his land, timber and related dealings, and once in Congress, Frank W. Boykin applied boundless energy to representing his district and the State of Alabama, and when his congressional career ended in 1962 he still maintained an active interest in politics while turning to his many business activities, and even at the end Frank W. Boykin was planning construction of a jet plane repair facility;

NOW, THEREFORE, BE IT RESOLVED BY THE LEGISLATURE OF ALABAMA, both Houses thereof concurring, that our heartfelt sympathy be extended to the family and friends of Congressman Frank W. Boykin of Mobile and directs that a copy of this resolution be spread upon the journal of the House and Senate and a copy sent to his family.

Approved May 14, 1969

Time: 12:31 P.M.

I hereby certify that the foregoing copy of an Act of the Legislature of Alabama has been compared with the enrolled Act and it is a true and correct copy thereof.

Given under my hand this 19th day of May 1969.

JOHN W. PEMBERTON

Clerk of the House

Frank Boykin continues today being remembered as an idol to the family and also to those of all colors, including white and black alike, whose hope was centered in him.

If we could throw back the white robe around the throne of God, we would see him leaning on Jesus, saying, "Come home, loved ones, weep not for me."

Friends, he is not dead; he is bigger than life as his memories live on and on into the third and fourth generations and beyond with his world-famous saying, "Everything's Made for Love."

CHAPTER TWENTY-FOUR

Post Commentaries

On February 20, 1958, the following telegram was perhaps the last one sent by all his living children to Congressman Boykin in Washington, D.C.:

A few years ago in Bladen Springs, the world was given promise of many good things, A Boykin lad was born and given Frank as His name, by the time you were ten, evidence was you would have fame for all the county was agog at his vim. He killed 40 rabbits one night for the price of them, before he reached 12, he was well on his way. As he worked like a man, with no time to play at 16 his business was cross ties and stores along with at least a hundred other chores. Then he bought land and built lots of ships. Everything Is Made for Love was heard from his lips. With all his fellowmen he walked hand in hand, and he married the most beautiful girl in the land. Nothing could stop them as this was a team. So, he then ran for Congress in the midst of a dream. To help all in need with his dynamic power. Like the Rock of Gibraltar. He's there liked a tower. So it is, with a great deal of pride, that we pay tribute to you and to all we confide, that we are the lucky ones who know you as Dad. As children of Frank Boykin, we've been very glad. We love you; we love you, and we like you, too. Our wish is this: When we all are full of Rigor, you'll still be here with all of your vigor. Happy Birthday.
The Boykin Children

Over fifty years later, on March 7, 2009, Grace Boykin held a book signing at the lodge in Double Gates, Alabama, for her book *Southern Hunt*, based on her research about the life of her esteemed and beloved grandfather, Frank W. Boykin. At it, she recited this poem:

> Count your garden by flowers,
> Never by leaves that fall.
> Count your days by golden hours,
> Don't remember clouds at all.
> Count your nights by stars, not shadows,
> Count your life by smiles, not tears,
> And with joy, count your age by friends, not years.

This was written for Frank Love's beginning and end are always new. For "Everything is made for Love", And that's what everyone's dreaming of, A mate, and a boy his girl and a bride with her groom. Yes, "Everything is made for Love!" Every pair is made from God. A star its night and a cloud in the sky, the sun its moon, and for you it's I! If made for song, and birds, dogs, friends and all that I love especially God above!

She added, "My grandfather had more friends than you could count, and that is how I remember him."

RESOLUTIONS

May in 1913. Frank wrote:

"My darling I wonder if you will ever know how much I love you.
Ocllo, I love you madly, I am just wild to hold you in my arms, to look into those eyes I love so dearly and kiss you breathless.

It is so good to have somebody and just look at who I am loving!

You're just what I've always needed. I have to come and get you. Ocllo, I can't do without you. It's awful to be separated.

Ocllo, for goodness sake write to me when I can come. I love you so, darling, I love, love, love you and nobody else but "OO."

I could write a million pages, Always forever, Your Frank.

We made it over fifty years of wedded bliss even when I flirted with others. You have always been the teacher in my life and stood by my side through thick and thin. I will wait for you in Heaven as I know our faith will both see us in Heaven and our spirits will live on together!

> Everything's Made For Love
> Let every good fellow now join in a song,
> Everythings made for Love:
> Success to each other and pass it along,
> Everything's made for Love:
>
> A friend on the left and a friend on the right,
> Everything's made for Love:
> In willing endeavor our hands we unite,
> Everything's Made for Love:

Should time or occasion compel us to part,
Everything's Made For Love:
These days shall ever enliven the heart,
Everything's Made for Love!

Vive la: Viva La: Vive l'Amour!
Vive la: Viva La: Vive l'Amour!
Vive La! Vive La! Vive l'Amour!
Everything's made for love:

As these may be my last words to you.
Will see you as a spirit in Heaven!

HARRY F. BYRD, FOR PRESIDENT
FRANK W. BOYKIN, FOR VICE PRESIDENT

JULY 11, 1948

Alabama has taken the lead in the Southern States in setting a pattern in resentment of the National Democratic Party's action as well as the policy as set forth by President Tru-man. I understand that this Pre-Convention caucus of all the Southern States is for the purpose of all the Southern States trying to get together to nominate some capable and qualified man for the Presidency who will respect the Southern States as to Civil Rights, Poll Tax, lynching, etc.

I see by the Press that General Eisenhower continues to decline to run for the nomination for President of the United States on the Democratic platform.

recently where he said he would not accept the nomination if given him and that he intended to vote for Mr. Dewey for President. It looks very much like we are wasting a lot of time and wistful thinking regarding General Eisenhower. I further understand that there is deposited in a safety deposit box in New York Central Patton's memoirs and criticism of General Eisenhower, and particularly regarding the Battle of the Bugle.

General Patton, I understand, requested that this information never be published or made public unless General Eisenhower tried to capitalize on his military reputation, and if he ever did that the memoirs and facts would be made public and that General Eisenhower would be credited with the blunders that happened in Europe from a military standpoint and especially the Battle of the Bulge and the continuation of the war which cost many thousands of lives.

Such a publication or information made public (if such information exists and is correct) would be very effective for the simple reason that nearly every voting home was touched by this war. If they did not have somebody in their own immediate family, they had some relations who were in Europe and especially those homes that lost sons would certainly be affected by such information being made public. I am simply telling you this for what it is worth. I cannot confirm it, neither can I deny it. It has been gossiped for the past year and I received it on very good authority.

Alabama is in a unique position, as I see it. They cannot afford to make a blunder or a mistake at this convention.

Alabama has set the pattern for the Southern States, and

as I understand, South Carolina, Mississippi and Arkansas have adopted Alabama's policy. I am not exactly clear on this, but I have been so advised. Since we have set the pattern, and we are going to try to endeavor to get the other Southern States to go along with us, why shouldn't Alabama take the lead with the other Southern States and nominate a man from the Southern States? In my opinion, the South and West are going to save the Democratic party. In the years past we have always been there. To my knowledge, and I do not know if my history is correct, Alabama has always been in the Democratic ranks.

We have never faltered. Yet a lot of the States that are having so much to say and are fixing up the Civil Rights platform have been the States that have been in and out. Some years they would be Democratic, some years they would be Republicans, yet we have always been in the Democratic column and yet we have to be dictated to and we have to listen to these in-and-out States.

I think there is just as good material in the South for the Presidency and Vice-presidency of the United States as there is in any State or any corner or any nook in the whole United States.

I would like to see our Delegation go to Philadelphia, prepared to offer the names of a Presidential. and Vice-presidential candidate to the other Southern States.

My mind is fixed on these two men. I would be agreeable to change with the majority; however, I do not believe that you can select a better team than I am going to mention in this letter and before mentioning them, I am going to give you my reasons for thinking they are a winning team.

FIRST: We have got to nominate a man who is nationally known, who is a statesman and who is qualified to be the President of the United States. We have got to select a man that some of the Republicans will vote for. There has never been a Republican President elected in this country unless a good many Democrats voted for him and vice versa, we have never elected a Democratic President unless the Republicans voted for him. How do the people think Mr. Roosevelt got the big majority vote he got unless a lot of Republicans voted for him?

Therefore, I am for naming a man who can receive the Republican vote from Republicans who cannot vote for Mr. Dewey. This is the first requisite that I have in mind in regard to nominating a President of the United States.

SECOND: A very important requisite in nominating a President of the United States is a man that would do honor to Alabama or any State that would nominate him, a man that is capable, a man that is a statesman, a man that would command respect, not only in Alabama or in his home State, but in every State in the Union.

THIRD: We should put up a man before this Southern group that would receive the unanimous vote from the entire Southern Delegation.

There would be no quibbling over him, and the entire Southern States Delegation would vote for him unanimously and stay with him throughout the balloting.

FOURTH: If we are the first on the roll call and we nominate such a man and his name is put before the convention for ballot, I can see no reason why we cannot vote for him and remain in the Convention and not vote for Truman and stay in that convention and fight for the nomination of our candidate.

FIFTH: If we do not go in there with a nominee that Alabama can support and Mr.

Truman's name is put up for nomination, then I am one of the fourteen (14) that is going to get up and walk out of the Convention. I do not want to walk out of the Convention. I want to go up there and fight for the nomination of a man that will do credit to the State of Alabama and all of the States of the United States.

SIXTH: The man that I want to name is Senator Harry Byrd of Virginia, who is already the Senator of the Mother of States and who has shown himself throughout his political career as a fearless, courageous Statesman. He is my type of man whom I know all about from his record, and I do not know if Mr. Eisenhower is a Democrat or a Re-publican, and I further do not know his stand on Civil Rights, FEPC, etc.; therefore, I cannot support Mr. Eisenhower under these conditions when he still says he will not accept the nomination and will vote the Republican ticket. What is the use if the people just keep on talking about it? Let's forget about it and get a man from the Southern States.

For the Vice-president nominee, I would suggest the greatest campaigner in all America to work as a team with Senator Byrd. This man is Congressman Frank W. Boykin from the First District of Alabama. There is no better campaigner in the United States Than frank Boykin. If you would give him time enough and it depended upon his campaign, he could be President of the United States himself.

What I mean by that is if Frank Boykin could see enough people and make enough speeches he could win more votes than any man I have ever known or seen. Frank Boykin has been tried. We know what kind of a man he is. We have his voting record. We have his records of accomplishments at Washington. He does not ask you what County you are from when you ask him for help.

He has been a Congressman for everybody in the whole State of Alabama. He is for Alabama and he is for the South. His voting record will also disclose his thinking. I was talking to Frank on the telephone in the last day or two and he told me that the Texas Delegation wanted to give him their fifty-three (53) votes for Vice-president of the United States. Frank did not tell me he was even a candidate. He just mentioned it to me in discussing with me some other matters. Frank Boykin does not know that I am writing this letter. Frank Boykin does not know that I am even suggesting his name with Senator Byrd as Vice-president of the United States.

With all the dissension about Mr. Truman, with Alabama having the first crack at this thing and nominating two (2) Southern men, I think that it would block Mr. Truman and I think throughout the balloting that our ticket would gain. I don't think that Mr.

Eisenhower would accept the nomination from all I know and I don't know how Mr. Eisenhower stands. I don't know whether we would have another Harry Truman so far as the South is concerned. This, I want someone to show me very plainly. I do know where Harry Byrd and Frank Boykin stand and I am willing to lose with them rather than win with somebody else, especially a Truman type.

While we might lose this National election, what we do now is going to have its effect in the future, and I think that we from the South should look at this matter, not so much in the light of just getting somebody to win, but in the light of getting the right people nominated. I am more of a good Democrat than I am a National party Democrat. I mean by that I would rather lose my man and vote for the right man than to win with a YELLOW DOG.

I am not an orator. I am just a plain, ordinary businessman, but if the Delegation from Alabama will just follow my suggestion and will put Mr. Byrd's name before the Southern States at their Pre-convention meeting and also the name of Frank Boykin and they would be acceptable to this group, it will be my great pleasure and privilege , if I was allowed such, to make the nominating speech before this Convention. That is where I again go off halfcocked as I do not know the procedure and this honor may come to our Chairman. However, if I was given the privilege and the right to do it, it would certainly be a great privilege to do so.

I also feel, regardless of what other States may do in regard to Mr. Eisenhower, that I would Jike to see Alabama nominate a Southern ticket.

Right along in this connection, there has been the name of Governor Laney of Arkansas mentioned. There has been the name of Governor Johnson of South Carolina mentioned.

No doubt, both of these are good men. However, I think that Senator Byrd is the most nationally known and is head and shoulders above everybody we have from the South today in the Democratic party. With placards they were nominated by a delegation from the floor of the House but lost as the National nominees for the Democratic Party.

Milton Keynes UK
Ingram Content Group UK Ltd.
UKHW022146111124
451073UK00007B/217